Good Morning Baking!

Good Morning Baking!

MANI NIALL   *photographs by* ERIN KUNKEL

EGG&DART®

Acknowledgments

Where can I begin thanking the many people that make a cookbook possible? A very special thanks to Publisher Pamela Falk for her wonderful excitement and belief in the concept that led to *Good Morning Baking!* Heartfelt thanks go to Leslie Jonath for pulling together all the pieces and making this book possible. I adore you. Everyone that has worked with me on this book has been the best supporter, encourager and taster—even from afar! Thanks to the entire team: Lisa McGuinness for your tireless attention to detail, Gretchen Scoble for the most delightful design, photographer Erin Kunkel and stylist Karen Shinto for your absolutely delectable images, Laurel Leigh for helping me get through the editorial process, Andrea Burnett for all your outreach and promotion. Steve Mounce, where would I be without you in the kitchen? Thanks for making this book, and the bakery, the best it can be.

Text copyright © 2013 by Mani Niall.
Photographs copyright © 2013 by Erin Kunkel.

ISBN 978-0-9838595-7-4

Manufactured in China

Designed and typeset by Gretchen Scoble.

10 9 8 7 6 5 4 3 2 1

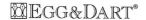 EGG&DART®
www.egganddartpress.com

This book is dedicated to the memory of my father,
George Brendan Nial, Sr., whose idea of a good morning began
with soft scrambled eggs, crisp bacon, and black coffee.
Please pass the biscuits!

Table of Contents

Introduction

Breakfast was the first meal I was allowed to cook on my own. *Allowed* might not be the right word, as I don't remember actually asking. I simply started cooking. It was probably after a sleepover in the fifth or sixth grade, and I imagine that by the time my friend and I got up, breakfast was done and my parents were finished cooking. You sleep in, you make your own! So I did.

I come from a family that cooked, so my taking action wasn't a surprise. My mom made dinner most nights, and all birthday cakes were homemade. My dad occasionally prepared some of the dishes he had tasted in France as a soldier during World War II, and my mom and dad collaborated on weekend brunches: they both liked their eggs soft scrambled, their bacon crisp, and hearty whole-grain or crusty breads. My mom made her own preserves, with big chunks of fruit and never too much sugar. It was only natural that both my sisters were comfortable in the kitchen, and as the youngest child in the family, I eagerly gobbled up their cookies and pound cakes.

I probably made pancakes from a mix that morning and cooked them in our electric skillet. I still like the steady heat of an electric skillet for pancakes, but these days I make my own batter from scratch. By high school, I had attempted muffins, and I recall a carrot-cake loaf that I made for a school bake sale. I think I goofed on the measurement for the oil, but instead of the cake

being a failure, everyone sincerely commented on how "moist" it was! I learned two things from that experience: I had a knack for this baking thing, and I had better read recipes more carefully.

Breakfast is a good entry point into the craft of baking. Most of the recipes are not too complex, and many do not require electric mixers or other tools and techniques that might put off novice bakers. Waking up to a delicious treat that is only minutes from a hot oven is a great way to start the day, to relax on the weekend, or to show folks you care. If you are a houseguest, baking demonstrates gratitude and can help to ensure you will be invited back. My grandparents' cabin on Payette Lake, in McCall, Idaho, was surrounded by huckleberry bushes. Come late July and August, we kids were sent out into the yard to pick a handful of the luscious, tart purply berries for the pancake batter. By the time they had eaten the pancakes, our houseguests were clamoring for a repeat invitation.

When I started college, I was working part-time in an Oregon natural foods restaurant, a classic old-school place in the tradition of New York's renowned Moosewood (which remains one of the few of that style founded in the 1970s that is still in business). There was very little access to the wide variety of high-quality, minimally processed ingredients that we take for granted today. The restaurant was fortunate to form a partnership with a natural foods distributor, which allowed it to acquire all types of raw nuts and seeds for making the house granola, as well as whole-grain flours, honey, locally produced dairy products, and other ingredients for baking. For example, it was almost impossible to find something like preservative-free unsweetened dried coconut in those days, yet the restaurant was able to acquire natural dried coconut, ground, grated, or ribboned!

My passion for food overtook my focus on studies, and I moved to Los Angeles to run the kitchen of our sister restaurant, the Golden Temple, at Third and Fairfax (now closed). The Source on Sunset Strip (famously lampooned by Woody Allen in *Annie Hall*) and the Golden Temple were the two stalwarts of the 1960s and 1970s health food movement. By the mid-1980s, the Los Angeles food scene had shifted. The focus was now on American ingredients, and an appreciative audience for delicious and authentic regional food had gathered. Chefs could no longer rely solely on a stodgy approach to "pure" cooking. They had to balance it with an equal focus on the aesthetics of taste, texture, and presentation.

Our customers at the Golden Temple ran the gamut from actresses and health food enthusiasts who subsisted on our salad bar to foodies who loved our authentic cooking (such as our traditional New Mexican chile sauce; more on that later) to families trying to find more healthful foods that their kids would eat. But the one thing that they all had in common was that they loved baked goods. I was fortunate to join a team that included chef-restaurateur Akasha Richmond, who nudged our customers away from carob cake to her house-made chocolate ganache, causing sales

to triple. We revised our corn bread, keeping the stone-ground cornmeal and millet for texture but replacing the whole-wheat flour with unbleached all-purpose flour to lighten the loaf considerably. Offered alongside our salad bar, that corn bread probably kept plenty of actresses from starving. It's still my favorite corn bread recipe.

A chance referral from Gurmukh Khalsa, the restaurant's manager and founder of the renowned Golden Bridge Yoga studios, set my life on a crash course on both cooking and baking over the next several years. One day she mentioned that Michael Jackson had started eating at the restaurant and really liked the food. But he was too busy at a nearby recording studio to come in as often as he would like, so he wanted to know if someone could start bringing him food. That someone was me, and within a few months, I was dropping off lunch, catering dinners at Michael's house, and sending off a bundle of veggie burgers and organic brownies with Paul and Linda McCartney as they boarded their Lear jet.

When Michael launched a tour two years after his wildly successful *Thriller* album, he asked me to come along as his private chef. The biggest thing I learned during that whirlwind experience? Baking can save any meal. It was not easy to cook in a new hotel kitchen in a different city every few days. Schedules changed constantly, and dinner guests arrived without notice. A bad breakfast at a hotel could be salvaged with a batch of freshly baked muffins. If I was expecting to serve one or two guests and I ended up with five, I had to be sure I had lots of homemade ice cream and cookies for dessert so that guests never left hungry. Michael's love of the smoky New Mexican red chile enchiladas he first tasted at the Golden Temple underscored the importance of ice cream: more than a few of his dinner guests were relieved to cool off after his favorite spicy meal. I had a special suitcase with me at all times that held the ice cream maker, a food processor, and all the specialty flours and spices I needed.

When I began working on Mani's Bakery, which I opened in Los Angeles a few years later, one thing became crystal clear: I had to bake something for everyone. Breakfast is a perfect example of this philosophy. While some people prefer to wake up with something sweet, others prefer a savory beginning. Some folks like whole grains, such as oatmeal or whole-wheat flour, and others want the flaky, buttery, and crisp texture that unbleached all-purpose flour delivers. Almost everyone likes lots of flavorful ripe fruit, chunky or creamy, and a vocal few favor chocolate.

That pretty much sums up my approach to baking, and it is what went in to creating this collection of recipes. You will occasionally find whole grains mixed with unbleached flour, but only if they contribute to the taste and texture of whatever I am making and definitely not if they make it clunky. There is a gluten-free recipe for blueberry corn muffins for anyone avoiding wheat or gluten, and I have included a few recipes that vegans can enjoy. When I bake for these special categories, first and foremost the food must taste good to whoever is eating it; otherwise, it doesn't make the final cut. Because I learned to bake with honey as the primary sweetener, I use it frequently, sometimes in conjunction with sugar. Honey keeps baked goods

moist, and you can buy it locally from beekeepers in your area. A handful of recipes are sweetened with such sugar alternatives as maple syrup and agave syrup. I am often asked about special diets and which of these sweeteners is "better" for you. I have cooked for just about every type of diet there is and realize that no single approach works for everyone. There are no magic solutions, foods, or diets.

Baking is for both sustenance and pleasure. The food we eat gives us calories, and calories are the fuel we need to keep our bodies running. Life is meant to be enjoyed, and nothing embodies this more than food enjoyed at the kitchen table, a place to sit and relax alone or with family or friends. Starting the day with fresh baked goods is a great way to connect with the world around you or to take some time for yourself. This is the idea behind my newest venture, Sweet Bar Bakery, located in a renovated candy factory in Oakland, California. Working in the kitchen, although often a solitary task, has opened many doors for me. Fortunately, people love to visit a bakery, so even though the hours are long, the rewards of preparing good food, making people happy, and having friends, family, and customers (old and new) visit daily are worth the time. I look forward to many more years of baking and invite you to find the same rewards in it that I have discovered: the same pleasure, lessons, and time well spent.

The Essential Kitchen

One thing that I have noticed from years of running a bakery is how important memory and consistency are to regular customers. People may dine at a beloved restaurant to see what new creations the chef has come up with, but when they go to a bakery, they want their favorite muffin or coffee cake to taste just as good as it did on the last visit, whether it was last month or last year. This is not to say that customers have no desire to try new items or seasonal specialties. But their sense memories are what tell them if the bakers are paying attention, if they are honoring their craft by bringing the same high level of detail and skill each and every day they bake. Part of that consistency comes from sourcing quality ingredients, working with them to get to know them, and then creating base formulas that are followed every time. Here are a few thoughts on finding the best ingredients for your home baking.

FLOURS AND GRAINS. Unbleached all-purpose flour is the go-to flour for the recipes here. I buy organic flour from a bulk bin for the best price. The flour is versatile, reliable, and conveys the flavor that most of us have come to expect from baked goods. Fortunately, it is also a great carrier for such add-ins as fruits, nuts, and whole grains. All-purpose flour is always yellowish when newly milled and bleaches naturally with time. Chemically bleaching the flour speeds up the process and alters the protein content slightly, making the formation of gluten more difficult. Try the various unbleached all-purpose flours available in your area and then, for consistent results, choose the one you prefer and stick to it!

When I first learned to bake, I was primarily using different types of whole-wheat flour, and the subtleties of whole-wheat pastry flour were a revelation. Although whole-wheat flour is great for some things, such as breads, breakfast bars, and some scones, it is entirely different from whole-wheat pastry flour. The latter, milled from soft wheat, is definitively a whole grain but does not have the large bran or germ particles and is slightly lower in both protein and gluten than regular whole-wheat flour, making it better for achieving the desired crumb in pastries. Be sure to check the label carefully to make sure you are purchasing whole-wheat *pastry* flour for many of the recipes here.

All whole-wheat flours have a tendency to go rancid faster than all-purpose flour because they have a higher oil content. (All-purpose flour contains the endosperm but the germ and bran are removed in milling, and whole-wheat flour includes all three components; the germ carries the oil.) To keep them fresh, I store them in tightly covered containers or resealable plastic bags in the freezer. In fact, that's the best way to store all whole grains, such as stone-ground cornmeal and rolled oats, both of which are also used in these pages.

Bread flour (made from hard wheat) has a higher protein content than all-purpose flour (made from a mixture of hard and soft wheats) and is used by bread and pizza bakers. I use it for making sweet yeast-leavened breakfast treats, such as cinnamon bread and snails, and certain biscuits and muffins. Semolina looks similar to cornmeal but is actually milled from durum wheat, the wheat most commonly used for making pasta. I fell in love with semolina loaves made by local artisanal bread bakers and began seeking out semolina for the color and texture it imparts in both sweet and savory baking. I use it in a scone recipe in this book. Be sure to purchase fine-grind semolina.

SWEETENERS. Granulated sugar is the sweetener most commonly called for in the following recipes. Just as with flour, I lean toward organic products and find the best price in larger packages or in the bulk bin at natural foods stores and upscale grocery stores. Make sure that the label says cane sugar rather than beet sugar, as the latter does not always caramelize well.

Keeping a variety of sugars on hand makes baking more fun, and unlike grains, they are not likely to go bad as long as they are tightly covered and stored at room temperature. Moisture is the main enemy of sugar. Home bakers typically keep granulated sugar and brown sugar on a cupboard shelf. Most brown sugar is refined granulated sugar with some of the molasses added back in, which makes it moister and gives it a caramel flavor. I find the difference between light and dark brown sugar to be minimal. Many of the recipes in this book calling for brown sugar do not indicate light or dark, so use what you have. Some do specify, but if a recipe calls for light brown sugar and you have only dark, go ahead and use it. It just means that the finished baked good will be slightly darker. And the reverse is true, of course, if you use light brown sugar in a recipe that calls for dark.

Turbinado and Demerara are brown sugars that are only minimally processed, which means they retain a small percentage of their natural molasses. They are drier than conventional brown sugar, have relatively large crystals (turbinado crystals are the larger of the two), and are used in these pages to make scones and as a topping because they retain their crunch better than granulated sugar. If you would like to experiment further, seek out muscovado sugar, a brown sugar produced by boiling the juice pressed from sugarcane without separating the molasses, creating a richer color, stronger flavor, larger crystals, and higher mineral content than turbinado or Demerara.

Honey in all its varieties is also a favorite sweetener of mine. The best honeys typically come from local or national artisanal beekeepers who harvest the honey when the bees are pollinating a specific crop. These honeys are often pricey and are best for slathering on your baked goods rather than using them in cooking. For baking, I buy honey in bulk and look for lighter-colored varieties. Color is an indicator of taste, with darker honeys tending to taste stronger.

Maple syrup and agave syrup (also known as agave nectar), both of which are easy to find in natural foods stores and in some supermarkets, are also used in this book. Pure maple syrup has a distinctive taste that I like, so I buy the brands with the best prices, often selecting grade A medium or dark or grade B for the best flavor. The term *grade* indicates the time of the harvest; grade A syrup, a product of the first harvest, has a mild flavor and light color. Agave syrup, which is harvested from the plant of the same name, is also available either light (amber) or dark. I like it for its neutral taste, minimal processing, and low position on the glycemic index. I prefer darker maple syrup and light agave syrup, but either will work in the recipes here, so choose according to your preference.

I also occasionally use unsulfured molasses as a sweetener. It is the syrup left over in sugar making once the crystals have formed. It comes in three types, light, dark, and blackstrap, from the first, second, and third boiling of the sugarcane juice, respectively. As the color darkens, the flavor intensifies and the viscosity increases. Any of the three types can be used in my recipes.

DAIRY PRODUCTS AND EGGS. I try to call for ingredients that people typically have on hand, such as yogurt rather than sour cream or buttermilk. The acidity of yogurt helps develop a tender crumb, much like buttermilk does, plus it is thick and has a rich mouthfeel that recalls sour cream. You can mix and match a bit as you like. For example, buttermilk is by definition low in fat, and I always use whole-milk yogurt, so if you are watching your fat intake, you can sometimes substitute buttermilk for yogurt. Skip nonfat yogurt for baking, as it does not hold up well. If you want a richer flavor in your coffee cakes, you can substitute sour cream for yogurt. Low-fat or whole milk will work fine in place of buttermilk in muffin recipes, though you may need a tablespoon less, as buttermilk is much thicker than milk. I always use whole milk in recipes calling for milk. Low-fat and nonfat milk lack the "body" needed to develop a good mouthfeel.

Nowadays, the egg sections of markets offer so many choices that selecting a carton can sometimes be a bit overwhelming. I buy large eggs, generally organic or cage free. I do not specify the size in recipes because it does not make a difference most of the time. If you decide to triple a recipe, however, be sure to use large eggs to avoid too much liquid. In some recipes, I call for eggs at room temperature. This is because when you beat them, they will take on more volume than eggs straight from the refrigerator. The batter will also rise better in the oven, especially if the recipe calls for several eggs. If you did not plan ahead, you can pop cold eggs into a bowl of very warm, not hot, water for about ten minutes before using them. If room-temperature eggs are not indicated in a recipe, cold eggs are fine.

Finally, I always use unsalted butter. If you see it on sale at the market, stock up on it and store it in the freezer. It will keep for a few months.

SPICES AND SALT. Try to purchase your spices in bulk at a natural foods store or other specialty

shop. It will allow you to buy just what you need. How many times have you looked at a large jar on your spice shelf and realized that you haven't opened it in two years? The oils in spices are volatile, so buying spices in small amounts means that they are more likely to be fresh when you use them, and fresh spices ensure that your baked goods will have better flavor. Cardamom is a good example. I never buy it already ground because it is one of the most volatile spices and loses its potency quickly once it is ground. Buy the seeds or pods, then separate the seeds from the husk if necessary and grind the seeds in a spice grinder as needed. I have added cardamom as an alternative spice in a handful of recipes because I believe it deserves a prominent spot alongside cinnamon, ginger, nutmeg, and the like.

Nutmeg, which is the hard, round, aromatic seed of the nutmeg tree, is an easy spice to use fresh. Keep a few whole nutmegs in your cupboard and you will always be able to freshly grate what you need for a recipe. I have not specified freshly grated nutmeg in my recipes, but if you have whole nutmegs on hand, use them. You may find that you need a bit less nutmeg than what is called for, as the flavor will be more potent.

I use fine sea salt in my baking recipes. You can use regular table salt as well. Kosher salt is much coarser than fine sea salt or table salt, which means that its volume measure is 1½ to double the amount of fine sea salt. If you opt to use kosher salt because you prefer the heightened taste it delivers to baked goods, be sure to adjust the amount accordingly.

Coffee cakes and their brethren, such as buckles and crisps, always remind me of the weekend breakfasts at home when I was growing up. We didn't have the fancy brunches we know today, nor did we call weekend breakfasts that, but there was generally something sweet on the table, and it was often the centerpiece of the meal. Occasionally it was picked up from a bakery or the grocery store, but I was much more interested when it was made at home. I would watch the recipe take shape, the measurements and the mixing, the pans being prepared and then filled with batter, and then wait impatiently until the item emerged from the oven. I could barely contain my enthusiasm.

At Sweet Bar Bakery, I have a team of bakers who are up early in the morning to make sure that all the baked goods are ready when the first customers walk in the door. But when I bake at home for family or guests who have spent the night, I like to measure the ingredients the evening before. Then I get up a bit before the others so that I can pop my treasure into the oven and let the wonderful aroma from the baking awaken everyone else.

In general, the baked goods in this chapter can be tightly covered and stored at room temperature for at least three days. If I want to keep them longer than that, I wrap them and freeze them for future reheating and serving. They will keep in the freezer for a couple of weeks.

Coffee Cakes, Buckles, Crisps & Puddings

Raspberry-Ginger Coffee Cake

Fresh ginger and honey add notes of spice and warmth to this simple yet rich coffee cake. Feel free to substitute your favorite freshly picked summer berry for the raspberries. Planning a special gathering? You can make the batter and streusel topping the day before (see note) to cut down on last-minute work on the day of the party. **MAKES 12 TO 15 SERVINGS**

2 cups unbleached all-purpose flour

1 teaspoon baking powder

½ teaspoon baking soda

½ teaspoon salt

½ cup (1 stick) unsalted butter, at room temperature

½ cup light-colored honey

½ cup firmly packed brown sugar

2 eggs, lightly beaten

Grated zest of 1 large orange (about 2 tablespoons)

2 to 3 teaspoons peeled and grated or minced fresh ginger

1 cup plain whole-milk yogurt

1½ cups fresh or frozen raspberries

1. Position a rack in the center of the oven and preheat to 350°F. Butter a 9-by-13-inch baking pan.

2. To make the cake, in a medium bowl, sift together the flour, baking powder, baking soda, and salt. In a large bowl, using a stand mixer fitted with the paddle attachment or a handheld mixer, cream together the butter, honey, and brown sugar on medium speed until smooth and creamy, about 3 minutes. Slowly add the eggs and beat until incorporated. Stop the mixer and scrape down the sides of the bowl.

3. On low speed, add half of the flour mixture and beat until blended. Stop the mixer and scrape down the sides of bowl. Again on low speed, add the orange zest, ginger, and yogurt and beat until thoroughly combined, then increase the speed to medium as the ingredients are incorporated to ensure even mixing and full absorption. Finally, on low speed, add the remaining flour mixture and beat until incorporated. Stop the mixer and scrape down the sides of the bowl to ensure all the ingredients are evenly mixed. Then, on medium speed, beat until the batter is smooth and creamy, about 30 seconds. Using a rubber spatula, fold in the raspberries. Spread the batter evenly in the prepared pan.

4. To make the streusel, in a medium bowl, toss together the brown sugar, flour, cinnamon, salt, and nuts. Scatter the butter over the top and work it in with your fingers until the mixture resembles coarse crumbs. Sprinkle the streusel evenly over the batter.

continued >

STREUSEL

¼ cup firmly packed brown sugar

¼ cup unbleached all-purpose flour

½ teaspoon ground cinnamon

¼ teaspoon salt

1¼ cups pecans or walnuts, chopped

5 tablespoons cold unsalted butter, cut into small pieces

5. Bake until a cake tester inserted into the center comes out clean, 35 to 45 minutes. Let cool at least slightly on a wire rack. Serve warm or at room temperature.

NOTE: You can make the batter as directed in steps 2 and 3, then cover the bowl tightly with plastic wrap and refrigerate it overnight. The next day, spread the batter in the prepared pan and let it sit at room temperature for about 30 minutes before baking. The streusel can also be made the day before and covered and stored at room temperature. Sprinkle it over the batter just before the pan goes into the oven.

Maple-Apple Streusel Coffee Cake

Calling all maple lovers! Apples and maple syrup are an ideal breakfast combination. For even more maple flavor, look for maple sugar, which is made by boiling down maple sap until it crystallizes, for the streusel topping. This large coffee cake will feed a crowd. Thanks to the maple syrup, any leftovers will stay moist and delicious tightly covered and stored at room temperature for up to 4 days. **MAKES 15 TO 18 SERVINGS**

3 cups unbleached all-purpose flour

1½ teaspoons baking soda

¾ teaspoon salt

1 teaspoon ground cinnamon

½ teaspoon ground ginger

¼ teaspoon ground allspice

1¼ cups maple syrup

1 cup buttermilk

3 eggs

½ cup canola or other neutral-flavored vegetable oil

2 medium-sized cooking apples such as Fuji or Granny Smith, halved, cored, and cut into small bite-sized chunks

STREUSEL

¾ cup maple sugar or firmly packed brown sugar

¾ cup old-fashioned rolled oats

¾ cup walnuts or pecans, chopped

4 tablespoons cold unsalted butter, cut into small pieces

1. Position a rack in the center of the oven and preheat to 350°F. Butter and flour a 9-by-13-inch baking pan.

2. To make the cake, in a large bowl, sift together the flour, baking soda, salt, cinnamon, ginger, and allspice. In a medium bowl, whisk together the maple syrup, buttermilk, eggs, and oil until well blended. Make a well in the flour mixture and pour in the maple syrup mixture. Using a wooden spoon, stir just until combined. Fold in the apple chunks. Spread the batter evenly in the prepared pan.

3. To make the streusel, in a medium bowl, stir together the sugar, oats, and nuts. Scatter the butter over the top and work it in with a fork or your fingers until the mixture forms crumbly lumps. Strew the streusel evenly over the batter.

4. Bake until the top springs back when pressed lightly in the center with a fingertip, 45 to 55 minutes. The top will color darker than many coffee cakes because of the maple syrup. Let cool slightly in the pan on a wire rack before serving.

Peach Breakfast Buckle

A buckle falls somewhere between a cobbler and a pudding cake and is so bursting with juicy fresh fruit that you don't mind it being a bit gooey and sticky. Use fresh peaches at the height of ripeness in summer. The rest of the year, use frozen peaches. Do not thaw them before folding them into the batter, but do toss an extra tablespoon of flour into the peach mixture. Frozen peaches will release more juice as they bake than fresh peaches, and the additional flour is needed to absorb the liquid. **MAKES 10 TO 12 SERVINGS**

1½ cups plus 2 tablespoons unbleached all-purpose flour

1 teaspoon baking powder

½ teaspoon baking soda

½ teaspoon salt

½ teaspoon ground nutmeg

½ teaspoon ground ginger

3 to 4 cups peeled, pitted, and sliced peaches (about 1½ pounds)

¾ cup plus 2 tablespoons granulated sugar

Juice of 1 lemon

½ cup (1 stick) cold unsalted butter

1 egg, lightly beaten

1 teaspoon vanilla extract

¾ cup whole milk

1. Position a rack in the center of the oven and preheat to 350°F. Butter and flour a 9-by-13-inch baking dish or spray with nonstick cooking spray.

2. To make the buckle, in a medium bowl, sift together the 1½ cups flour, the baking powder, baking soda, salt, nutmeg, and ginger. In a second medium bowl, stir together the peaches, the 2 tablespoons flour, the 2 tablespoons granulated sugar, and the lemon juice.

3. In a large bowl, using a stand mixer fitted with the paddle attachment or a handheld mixer, cream together the butter and the ¾ cup sugar on medium speed until smooth and creamy, about 3 minutes. Add the egg and vanilla and beat until combined. Don't worry if the mixture looks curdled at this point. Stop the mixer and scrape down the sides of the bowl.

4. On medium speed, add half of the flour mixture and beat until combined. Add the milk and continue to beat until incorporated. The mixture may again look curdled, but that's okay. Add the remaining flour mixture and beat until incorporated. Using a rubber spatula, fold the peach mixture into the batter.

5. Spread the batter evenly in the prepared pan. For the topping, scatter the pecans evenly over the batter, then the butter, and finally the brown sugar.

TOPPING

1 cup pecan halves or pieces

4 tablespoons cold unsalted
  butter, cut into small pieces

¼ cup firmly packed light
  brown sugar

6. Bake until the top is golden brown and the center springs back when lightly pressed with a fingertip, about 35 minutes. The amount of peaches makes using a cake tester to test for doneness difficult, because the center is often still crumbly and gooey even when done. Let cool for a few minutes on a wire rack, then serve warm.

Mexican Breakfast Bread Pudding

The best bread to use for this dish is a standard, soft (but not pillowy) French or Italian loaf. Don't use a rustic sourdough with a thick crust and a lot of interior air holes, as it won't soak up the syrup properly. Panela, also known as piloncillo, is a popular Latin American sugar made by boiling sugarcane juice to evaporate the liquid, then pressing the resulting crystals into a block or cone. To cut the sweetness, the pudding is served with sharp Manchego cheese and tangy sour cream. **MAKES 4 TO 6 SERVINGS**

6 tablespoons unsalted butter, melted

12 slices French or Italian bread, each 1 inch thick

2 cups grated panela or firmly packed dark brown sugar

3 (3-inch) cinnamon sticks, or ¾ teaspoon ground cinnamon

1½ teaspoons aniseeds

⅔ cup slivered blanched almonds

4 ounces Manchego or mild Cheddar cheese, thinly sliced, for serving

Crème fraîche or sour cream for serving

1. Position a rack in the center of the oven and preheat to 350°F. Lightly brush a 9-by-13-inch glass baking dish with a little of the melted butter.

2. Brush both sides of each bread slice with some of the melted butter and arrange them in a single layer on a baking sheet. Reserve the remaining butter. Bake the slices for 10 minutes. Turn the bread slices over and bake until golden and crisp, about 5 minutes longer. Remove from the oven and transfer the slices to the prepared baking dish, overlapping them as needed. Leave the oven on.

3. While the bread is the oven, in a medium saucepan, combine the panela, cinnamon sticks, aniseeds, reserved butter, and 1½ cups water and bring to a boil over medium-high heat, stirring just until the sugar dissolves. Boil uncovered, stirring occasionally, until reduced to 2 cups, about 15 minutes. Remove from the heat.

4. Moving a fine-mesh sieve evenly over the bread in the baking dish, slowly pour the warm syrup through the sieve, turning the bread over once the first side is saturated and allowing some of syrup to be absorbed before adding more. When all of the syrup has been added, sprinkle the almonds evenly over the top.

5. Cover the baking dish with aluminum foil. Bake the pudding until the syrup is bubbling, about 25 minutes. Remove from the oven and spoon the pudding into individual bowls. Top each serving with a slice or two of cheese and a dollop of crème fraîche. Serve hot.

Orange-Walnut Cake with Brown Sugar-Rum Syrup

This cake is loaded with high-protein, antioxidant-rich walnuts. That's good health news for me because I have always loved the taste of walnuts, especially when they are lightly toasted before they go into a batter or dough. If possible, use just a single large orange for both the zest for the cake and the juice for the syrup. Remove the zest gently so that you can cut the orange in half and squeeze the halves for the juice. **MAKES 12 SERVINGS**

2½ cups walnuts

1 cup granulated sugar

Grated zest of 1 large orange

2 eggs, at room temperature

¾ cup canola or other neutral-flavored vegetable oil

¼ cup light-colored honey

2½ cups unbleached all-purpose flour

1 teaspoon baking powder

1 teaspoon baking soda

1½ teaspoons ground cinnamon

½ teaspoon ground nutmeg

½ teaspoon salt

1½ cups boiling water

1. Position a rack in the lower third of the oven and preheat to 350°F. Butter and flour a 10- to 12-cup fluted tube or Bundt pan.

2. Spread the walnuts on a rimmed baking sheet and toast, stirring once midway through baking, just until they begin to release their fragrance, 10 to 12 minutes. Pour onto a plate and let cool. Leave the oven on.

3. To make the cake, combine the walnuts, ¼ cup of the granulated sugar, and the orange zest in a food processor and pulse about six times until the walnuts are very finely chopped but not a powder. Measure out 1¾ cups of the nut mixture for the cake and reserve the rest to use as a topping.

4. In a medium bowl, whisk the remaining ¾ cup granulated sugar with the eggs, oil, and honey. In a large bowl, sift together the flour, baking powder, baking soda, cinnamon, nutmeg, and salt. Make a well in the flour mixture and pour in the egg mixture. Whisk together the dry and wet ingredients, gradually adding the boiling water as you whisk. (Do not pour the boiling water directly onto the egg mixture, or the eggs may curdle.) Stir in the 1¾ cups nut mixture until combined. Spread the batter evenly in the prepared pan.

BROWN SUGAR—RUM SYRUP

⅔ **cup firmly packed light
brown sugar**

⅓ **cup dark rum**

⅓ **cup orange juice, preferably
freshly squeezed**

5. Bake until a cake tester inserted near the center comes out clean, 35 to 40 minutes. Let cool in the pan on a wire rack for about 20 minutes. Invert the pan onto the rack to unmold the cake, then lift off the pan.

6. While the cake is cooling, make the syrup. In a small saucepan, combine the brown sugar, rum, and orange juice over medium-low heat and bring just to a boil, stirring until the sugar dissolves. Cook at a gentle boil until slightly reduced, about 8 minutes. Remove from the heat.

7. Place a rimmed baking sheet under the rack holding the cake. Brush the top and the sides of the warm cake with the syrup in three applications, allowing about 5 minutes between the applications. Pour any glaze that falls onto the baking sheet back into the saucepan, reheat if necessary, and brush over the cake. When all of the syrup has been applied, place the cake, still on the rack, over a clean plate. Press handfuls of the reserved walnut mixture evenly over the top and sides of the cake, pressing the mixture firmly onto the cake. Let the cake cool completely, then cut into wedges to serve. (The cake can be placed in an airtight container or wrapped in plastic wrap and stored at room temperature for up to 5 days.)

Apricot-Cherry Breakfast Buckle

I first read about buckles in a Lee Bailey cookbook published before the advent of high-style food photography. The baked goods are seen cooling behind screen doors or being served in shady backyards, with blooming flowers overflowing the surrounding vines—the same relaxed summer mood this recipe brings to mind. **MAKES 10 TO 12 SERVINGS**

1¾ cups plus 2 tablespoons unbleached all-purpose flour

2 teaspoons baking powder

½ teaspoon salt

¾ cup (1½ sticks) unsalted butter, at room temperature

¾ cup sugar

2 eggs, lightly beaten

½ cup whole milk

1½ cups pitted and quartered apricots (about 8 apricots)

1½ cups pitted and halved fresh or frozen cherries (about 10 ounces)

TOPPING

⅓ cup sugar

¼ cup unbleached all-purpose flour

½ teaspoon ground cinnamon

4 tablespoons cold unsalted butter, cut into small pieces

1. Position a rack in the center of the oven and preheat to 350°F. Butter and flour a 9-inch springform pan or a 9-inch round cake pan with 2-inch sides.

2. To make the buckle, in a medium bowl, stir together the flour, baking powder, and salt. In a large bowl, using a stand mixer fitted with the paddle attachment or a handheld mixer, cream together the butter and sugar on medium speed until smooth and creamy, about 3 minutes. Add the eggs and beat until combined.

3. On low speed, add the flour mixture in three batches alternating with the milk in two batches, beginning and ending with the flour mixture. Beat well after each addition, increasing the speed to ensure even absorption, and stop and scrape the sides and bottom of the bowl occasionally to ensure even mixing. Using a wooden spoon, stir in the apricots and half of the cherries.

4. Spoon the batter into the prepared pan and smooth the top. Distribute the remaining cherries evenly over the batter, pressing them in gently. To make the topping, in a small bowl, whisk together the sugar, flour, and cinnamon, then scatter the butter over the top. Using a fork or your fingers, work in the butter until the mixture forms crumbly lumps. Scatter the topping over the cherries.

5. Bake until a cake tester inserted into the center comes out clean, about 55 minutes. Cool in the pan on a wire rack. If you have used a springform pan, unclasp, lift the sides off, and transfer the cake to a serving plate. If you have used a cake pan, serve directly from the pan.

Caramel Applesauce Cake

I love to confound expectations by serving tasty, healthful, delicious baked goods made from whole grains. The thin layer of rich and gooey caramel here achieves just that: it lifts a simple whole-grain applesauce and raisin cake to a new level. Why wait until fall for caramel apples? **MAKES ABOUT 15 SERVINGS**

2¾ cups whole-wheat pastry flour

2 teaspoons baking powder

1 teaspoon baking soda

2 teaspoons ground cinnamon

2 teaspoons ground ginger

½ teaspoon ground nutmeg

½ teaspoon salt

4 eggs, at room temperature

1¼ cups granulated sugar

1½ cups unsweetened applesauce

¾ cup canola or other neutral-flavored vegetable oil

1 cup raisins

CARAMEL TOPPING

1 cup firmly packed brown sugar

½ cup (1 stick) unsalted butter, cut into pieces

¼ cup whole milk

1. Position a rack in the center of the oven and preheat to 350°F. Butter and flour a 9-by-13-inch baking pan.

2. To make the cake, in a large bowl, sift together the flour, baking powder, baking soda, cinnamon, ginger, nutmeg, and salt. In a medium bowl, whisk together the eggs and granulated sugar, then add the applesauce and oil and whisk until well combined. Make a well in the flour mixture and pour in the applesauce mixture. Using a wooden spoon, stir just until combined. Fold in the raisins. Spread the batter evenly in the prepared pan.

3. Bake until the cake springs back when pressed gently in the center with a fingertip, 38 to 45 minutes. Let cool slightly on a wire rack.

4. While the cake is cooling, make the caramel topping. In a medium saucepan, combine the brown sugar, butter, and milk and bring to a boil over medium heat, stirring just until the sugar dissolves. Boil uncovered, stirring constantly, until the topping is bubbling and thickened, about 5 minutes.

5. Poke the surface of the warm cake all over with the thin tines of a fork. Pour the hot caramel topping evenly over the cake. If the caramel pools at the edges of the pan as it sets up, use an offset spatula to swirl it back to the center of the cake so that it can be absorbed. Let the cake cool completely before serving. (The cake can be covered with plastic wrap and stored at room temperature for up to 2 days. If desired, reheat individual pieces in a toaster oven, arranging them on a tray to capture the gooey caramel.)

Nectarine-Blackberry Crisp

This crisp is a delicious and foolproof way to showcase summer fruits. It is also gluten-free, although some oats are not truly gluten-free. Oats that are processed in a plant that also processes wheat can pick up a little gluten, so if you need to avoid even the smallest amount, look for rolled oats labeled "gluten-free," which means that they have been processed in a facility that does not process products containing gluten. For anyone not concerned with ingesting gluten, this recipe works equally well using 1½ cups of almost any type of flour, such as unbleached all-purpose, spelt, or whole-wheat pastry flour, along with the rolled oats.

MAKES ABOUT 12 SERVINGS

FRUIT LAYER

5 nectarines (about 2½ pounds), pitted and sliced

2 cups fresh or frozen blackberries

2 teaspoons grated orange zest

3 tablespoons sugar

4 teaspoons cornstarch

CRISP LAYER

1½ cups quick-cooking rolled oats

1½ cups gluten-free flour such as rice, buckwheat, or a gluten-free blend (see note)

⅔ cup sugar

½ teaspoon salt

½ cup (1 stick) plus 2 tablespoons cold unsalted butter

Heavy cream or half-and-half for serving (optional)

1. Position a rack in the center of the oven and preheat to 350°F. Have ready a 9-by-13-inch baking pan.

2. To make the fruit layer, in a large bowl, toss together the nectarines, berries, and orange zest. In a small bowl, stir together the sugar and cornstarch. Sprinkle the sugar mixture evenly over the fruit, then stir it in gently with a large spoon. Spread the fruit evenly in the pan.

3. To make the crisp layer, in a medium bowl, whisk together the oats, flour, sugar, and salt. Cut the ½ cup butter into small pieces and scatter the pieces over the oats mixture. Using a pastry blender or your fingertips, work in the butter until the mixture is crumbly. Scatter the mixture evenly over the fruit. Cut the 2 tablespoons butter into bits and dot the top with the butter.

4. Bake until the topping is evenly browned and the fruit toward the center of the pan is bubbling, about 45 minutes. Let cool on a wire rack for several minutes. Serve the crisp warm. For a special treat, douse each serving with a few tablespoons of cream.

NOTE: Be sure to use a gluten-free flour blend, not a gluten-free baking mix. The latter will contain leavening, which you do not need for this recipe.

Orange-Cardamom Coffee Cake

If you don't have a spice grinder or a spare coffee grinder, get one. Nothing beats the aroma and flavor of freshly ground cardamom. Failing that, seek out a natural foods store or other specialty shop that carries freshly ground cardamom in bulk. Even some grocery stores are beginning to carry good-quality spices in bulk. This allows you to buy spices in smaller amounts so that their volatile oils remain vividly fresh and aromatic. You won't regret the extra effort. **MAKES ABOUT 16 SERVINGS**

2 cups unbleached all-purpose flour

1 teaspoon baking powder

1 teaspoon baking soda

½ teaspoon salt

½ cup (1 stick) unsalted butter, at room temperature

½ cup light-colored honey

½ cup firmly packed light brown sugar

3 eggs, lightly beaten

1 tablespoon grated orange zest

2 teaspoons peeled and grated fresh ginger

1 cup sour cream

1. Position a rack in the lower third of the oven and preheat to 350°F. Butter and flour a 10- to 12-cup tube or Bundt pan.

2. To make the cake, in a medium bowl, sift together the flour, baking powder, baking soda, and salt. In a large bowl, using a stand mixer fitted with the paddle attachment or a handheld mixer, cream together the butter, honey, and brown sugar on medium speed until smooth and creamy, about 3 minutes. Add the eggs very slowly and beat until incorporated. As you add the eggs, stop the mixer once or twice and scrape down the sides of the bowl.

3. On low speed, add half of the flour mixture and beat until blended. Add the orange zest, the ginger, and the sour cream and beat until thoroughly mixed. Finally, add the remaining flour mixture and beat until combined. Stop the mixer after each addition and scrape the sides and bottom of the bowl to ensure the ingredients are evenly mixed, then increase the speed slightly and blend until the mixture is smooth. After the final addition, increase the speed to high and beat for about 30 seconds.

4. To make the streusel, in a medium bowl, toss together the brown sugar, flour, cinnamon, cardamom, allspice, salt, pepper, and nuts. Scatter the butter over the top and work it in with your fingers until the mixture resembles coarse crumbs. Stir in the orange zest.

STREUSEL

¼ cup firmly packed light brown
sugar

6 tablespoons unbleached
all-purpose flour

½ teaspoon ground cinnamon

1 teaspoon ground cardamom,
preferably freshly ground

¼ teaspoon ground allspice

¼ teaspoon salt

Pinch of freshly ground pepper

1¼ cups pecans or walnuts,
chopped

5 tablespoons cold unsalted
butter, cut into small pieces

1 tablespoon grated orange zest

5. Spread two-thirds of the batter evenly in the prepared pan and sprinkle with half of the streusel. Drop the remaining batter by spoonfuls evenly over the streusel layer, then smooth the surface of the batter. Sprinkle evenly with the remaining streusel.

6. Bake until a cake tester inserted near the center comes out clean, 45 to 50 minutes. Let cool in the pan on a wire rack for about 20 minutes. Invert the pan onto a plate to unmold the cake, then lift off the pan. Using a second plate, immediately turn the cake streusel side up. Serve warm or at room temperature.

Blueberry Polenta Cake

Blueberries are popular nowadays, and lemon always brings out their best flavor. This cake reheats wonderfully: just pop a slice into a toaster oven or a hot oven for a few minutes and the surface will recrisp, while the crumb remains as moist when it was freshly baked. **MAKES 8 TO 10 SERVINGS**

1½ cups unbleached all-purpose flour

½ cup stone-ground yellow cornmeal

1 teaspoon baking powder

½ teaspoon baking soda

½ teaspoon salt

½ cup (1 stick) unsalted butter, at room temperature

1 cup sugar

2 eggs, lightly beaten

Grated zest and juice of 1 lemon

1 cup sour cream

1¾ cups fresh or frozen blueberries

1. Position a rack in the center of the oven and preheat to 350°F. Brush a 9- or 10-inch cast-iron skillet with melted butter.

2. In a medium bowl, sift together the flour, cornmeal, baking powder, baking soda, and salt. Set aside. In a large bowl, using a stand mixer fitted with the paddle attachment or a handheld mixer, cream together the butter and sugar on medium speed until creamy and smooth, about 3 minutes. Slowly add the eggs and beat until incorporated. As you add the eggs, stop the mixer once or twice and scrape down the sides of the bowl.

3. On low speed, add half of the flour mixture and beat until incorporated. Add the lemon zest and juice and sour cream and beat until thoroughly mixed. Finally, add the remaining flour mixture and beat until combined. Stop the mixer after each addition and scrape the sides and bottom of the bowl to ensure the ingredients are evenly mixed, then increase the speed slightly and beat until the mixture is smooth. After the final addition, increase the speed to high and beat for about 30 seconds. Using a rubber spatula, fold in 1½ cups of the blueberries. Spread the batter in the prepared pan and smooth the top. Scatter the remaining ¼ cup berries evenly over the batter.

4. Bake the cake, rotating the pan back to front after about 30 minutes, until a cake tester inserted into the center comes out clean, about 45 minutes. Let cool in the pan on a wire rack for about 15 minutes, then run an offset spatula around the inside edge of the pan to loosen the cake sides. Serve warm.

Here you will find the home baker's answer to having plenty of freshly baked goods on hand. These recipes for tea cakes and quick breads are designed to keep you in stock for the better part of a week. They will keep tightly covered at room temperature unless otherwise noted. A few are sweetened with honey, which helps them remain moist. Several are loaded with chunks of fruit or with pureed banana or pumpkin, which also keeps them moist along with adding flavor. Glazes and toppings contribute to freshness and taste.

A good toaster oven, especially one with a convection option, is the best way to reheat baked goods. It heats the butter and other ingredients, crisping the surface and permeating the interior of the crumb with moisture so that the bread or cake tastes like it did when it first came out of the oven. This is especially true of the Bacon & Cheddar Corn Bread, but just about every recipe in this chapter benefits from toasting once it is a day old. If you are reheating leftover Pumpkin-Cranberry Tea Cake, Lemon–Poppy Seed Morning Bundt Cake, Ginger-Date-Pecan Bundt Cake, or Sweet Potato–Walnut Bread, add a dollop of cream cheese to the top of each piece before putting it in the toaster oven and you won't regret it. Always use a metal tray for heating to catch any gooey glazes.

Tea Cakes
&
Quick Breads

Bacon & Cheddar Corn Bread

This is corn bread the way it used to be made, and it calls for both bacon and rendered bacon fat for flavor. You can substitute vegetable oil for the bacon fat and skip the bacon if you like, or you can just think of the bacon and Cheddar cheese as two ways to put more protein in your diet. Any leftovers reheat nicely in a toaster oven. **MAKES 8 TO 10 SERVINGS**

5 slices bacon

2 cups stone-ground yellow cornmeal

½ cup unbleached all-purpose flour

3 tablespoons sugar

1 tablespoon baking powder

½ teaspoon baking soda

¾ teaspoon salt

1⅓ cups buttermilk

2 eggs, lightly beaten

1½ cups grated sharp Cheddar cheese

1. Preheat the oven to 425°F. While the oven is heating, cook the bacon in a 10-inch cast-iron skillet over medium-low heat, turning the slices a few times, until crisp. Transfer the bacon to paper towels to drain. Pour off the bacon fat from the pan and reserve; you should have 3 to 4 tablespoons. Crumble the bacon and reserve. Scrape up any browned bits stuck to the bottom of the skillet but do not rinse the pan. It will be used to bake the corn bread.

2. In a large bowl, sift together the cornmeal, flour, sugar, baking powder, baking soda, and salt. Make a well in the cornmeal mixture and pour in the buttermilk, eggs, and reserved bacon fat all at once. Whisk together the dry and wet ingredients until smooth. Using a rubber spatula, fold in the bacon and the cheese.

3. Pour the batter into the skillet (the pan will still be warm from frying the bacon). Bake until the corn bread springs back when lightly pressed in the center with a fingertip, 20 to 24 minutes. Cut into wedges and serve warm.

Banana-Chocolate Crunch Cake

Granola and bananas are among my favorite breakfast standbys. With that in mind, I wanted to make something that captured the crunch of granola and the creamy tropical taste of banana in a cake that was not too sweet. **MAKES 8 TO 10 SERVINGS**

1½ cups unbleached all-purpose flour

¾ teaspoon baking soda

½ teaspoon baking powder

½ teaspoon ground cinnamon

½ teaspoon ground ginger

⅛ teaspoon ground cloves

¼ teaspoon salt

¾ cup very smoothly mashed ripe banana (about 2 medium bananas)

1 cup agave syrup, preferably light

⅓ cup plus 2 tablespoons canola oil

1½ teaspoons vanilla extract

½ cup granola

½ cup semisweet chocolate chips

1. Position a rack in the center of the oven and preheat to 350°F. Brush a 9-inch round cake pan with 2-inch sides with oil or spray with nonstick cooking spray.

2. In a medium bowl, sift together the flour, baking soda, baking powder, cinnamon, ginger, cloves, and salt. In a second medium bowl, combine the banana, agave syrup, oil, and vanilla and whisk until well combined and smooth. Make a well in the flour mixture and pour in the banana mixture. Whisk together the dry and wet ingredients until smooth, scraping down the sides of the bowl with a rubber spatula as needed. Pour the batter into the prepared pan and smooth the top. Scatter the granola and chocolate chips evenly over the batter.

3. Bake until a cake tester inserted into the center comes out clean, about 30 minutes. Let cool on a wire cake rack for about 25 minutes. To keep the crunchy topping of granola and chocolate chips in place, you will need to invert the cake and then immediately turn it right side up on a serving plate. Here's how: Run a knife or offset spatula around the inside edge of the pan to loosen the cake sides. Invert the wire rack on top of the pan and then invert the pan and rack together. Tap the bottom of the pan to loosen the cake and then lift off the pan. With the rack still in place, turn the cake right side up, place on a serving plate, and then lift off the rack. Let cool completely before serving.

Pumpkin-Cranberry Tea Cake

This recipe is based on what was the best-selling muffin at Mani's Bakery for almost twenty years. It is plenty sweet enough, but using agave syrup, which is milder than sugar, allows the creamy pumpkin flavor and the tart berries to meld smoothly. It is hard to find fresh—or even frozen—cranberries except in the fall, so get them while you can. If you use frozen ones, do not thaw them before adding them to the batter.

MAKES 2 LOAVES

2½ cups unbleached all-purpose flour

1 teaspoon baking soda

½ teaspoon baking powder

½ teaspoon salt

½ teaspoon ground cinnamon

½ teaspoon ground ginger

¼ teaspoon ground allspice

¼ teaspoon ground nutmeg

3 eggs

1¼ cups pumpkin puree

½ cup canola or other neutral-flavored vegetable oil

1 cup agave syrup, preferably light

1½ cups fresh or frozen cranberries

1½ cups walnuts, chopped

1. Position a rack in the center of the oven and preheat to 375°F. Oil and flour two 8½-by-4½-by-2½-inch loaf pans or spray with nonstick cooking spray.

2. In a large bowl, sift together the flour, baking soda, baking powder, salt, cinnamon, ginger, allspice, and nutmeg. In a medium bowl, whisk the eggs vigorously until blended. Add the pumpkin, oil, and agave syrup and whisk until thoroughly combined.

3. Make a well in the flour mixture and pour in the egg mixture. Whisk together the dry and wet ingredients until blended. Do not overmix. Using a rubber spatula, fold in 1 cup each of the cranberries and walnuts. Divide the batter evenly between the prepared pans. Scatter the remaining ½ cup *each* cranberries and nuts evenly over the tops, pushing them gently into the batter to help them adhere and prevent burning.

4. Bake until the tops of the cakes spring back when pressed lightly in the center with a fingertip, 45 to 50 minutes. Let cool in the pans on wire racks for about 20 minutes. Run a knife around the inside edge of each pan to loosen the cake sides, then unmold the cakes onto the racks. Let cool completely before serving.

Traditional Glazed Honey Cake

It is difficult to apply the usual tests for doneness when baking this cake. It should spring back when pressed lightly with a fingertip, but the center tends to be a bit gooey even when the cake is done. My advice? Set the timer, pour yourself an extra cup of coffee, and enjoy a nice, quiet moment while you wait.

MAKES ABOUT 15 SERVINGS

1½ cups pitted prunes (dried plums)

½ cup ruby port

2 cups unbleached all-purpose flour

1 teaspoon baking powder

1 teaspoon baking soda

½ teaspoon ground nutmeg

½ teaspoon ground allspice

½ teaspoon salt

½ cup (1 stick) unsalted butter, at room temperature

½ cup sugar

½ cup light-colored honey

1½ teaspoons vanilla extract

3 eggs, lightly beaten

¾ cup whole-milk plain yogurt

1. Chop the prunes coarsely into thirds. In a medium bowl, combine the prunes and port and let soak, stirring the mixture occasionally, for at least 2 hours or up to overnight. Drain just before using.

2. Position a rack in the center of the oven and preheat to 350°F. Butter and flour a 9-by-13-inch baking pan.

3. To make the cake, in a medium bowl, sift together the flour, baking powder, baking soda, nutmeg, allspice, and salt. In a large bowl, using a stand mixer fitted with the paddle attachment or a handheld mixer, cream together the butter and sugar on medium speed until creamy and smooth, about 2 minutes. With the mixer running, slowly pour in the honey over the course of about 2 minutes. As you add the honey, stop the mixer and scrape down the sides of the bowl two or three times to ensure the ingredients are evenly mixed. Add the vanilla, then slowly add the eggs over the course of 2 minutes and beat until incorporated, again stopping the mixer and scraping the bowl as needed. The mixture may look lumpy or slightly curdled, and that's okay.

4. On low speed, add half of the flour mixture and beat until fully incorporated. Add the yogurt and mix until thoroughly combined. Finally, add the remaining flour mixture and beat until incorporated. Stop and scrape the sides and bottom of the bowl between additions to ensure all the ingredients are evenly mixed, and increase the speed briefly after each addition until the mixture is smooth and creamy.

GLAZE

3 tablespoons light-colored honey

3 tablespoons sugar

2 tablespoons whole milk

2 tablespoons unsalted butter

1 teaspoon ground cinnamon

After the final addition, mix on high speed for about 30 seconds to ensure all the ingredients are well mixed. Drain the prunes, then, using a rubber spatula, fold them into batter. Spread the batter evenly in the prepared pan and smooth the top.

5. To make the glaze, in a small saucepan, combine the honey, sugar, milk, butter, and cinnamon and bring to a rolling boil over medium heat, stirring constantly. Remove from the heat and spread the glaze evenly over the batter.

6. Bake until the top of the cake springs back when pressed lightly in the center with a fingertip, about 35 minutes. Let cool briefly on a wire rack, then serve warm.

Lemon-Poppy Seed Morning Bundt Cake

Mixing the sweetness of honey and the tang of fresh lemons is a great way to start the day. Use a light-colored honey, or use creamed honey for its ease in blending, pale color, and milder flavor. This cake often bakes up two-toned, honey brown fading to lemon yellow. **MAKES 12 TO 16 SERVINGS**

3 cups unbleached all-purpose flour

2½ teaspoons baking powder

½ teaspoon baking soda

½ teaspoon salt

1 cup (2 sticks) unsalted butter, at room temperature

1⅓ cups orange blossom or other light-colored honey

5 eggs, lightly beaten

1 teaspoon vanilla extract

⅔ cup whole milk

Grated zest of 2 large lemons (about 2 tablespoons)

2½ tablespoons poppy seeds

1. Position a rack in the lower third of the oven and preheat the oven to 350°F. Butter and flour a 10- to 12-cup Bundt or fluted tube pan.

2. To make the cake, in a medium bowl, sift together the flour, baking powder, baking soda, and salt. In a large bowl, using a stand mixer fitted with the whip attachment or a handheld mixer, cream together the butter and honey on low speed, increasing to medium speed until smooth, about 3 minutes. Slowly add the eggs and beat until incorporated. As you add the eggs, stop the mixer and scrape down the sides of the bowl a few times. The mixture may look curdled, which is okay. Add the vanilla and beat until combined.

3. On low speed, add the flour mixture in three batches alternating with the milk in two batches, beginning and ending with the flour mixture. Stop and scrape the sides and bottom of the bowl between additions to ensure all the ingredients are evenly mixed, and increase the speed briefly after each addition until the mixture is smooth and creamy. After the final addition, mix on high speed for about 30 seconds to ensure all the ingredients are well mixed. Using a rubber spatula, fold in the lemon zest and poppy seeds. Spread the batter evenly in the prepared pan and smooth the top.

GLAZE

⅓ **cup freshly squeezed lemon juice**

3 **tablespoons orange blossom or other light-colored honey**

Confectioners' sugar for dusting (optional)

4. Bake until a cake tester inserted near the center of the cake comes out clean, about 45 minutes. Start checking for doneness at 40 minutes. Let cool in the pan on a wire rack for 20 minutes.

5. Make the glaze while the cake is cooling. In a small bowl, whisk together the lemon juice and honey.

6. After the cake has cooled for 20 minutes, invert the pan onto the rack to unmold the cake, then lift off the pan. Slide a large, flat plate under the rack holding the still-warm cake and immediately brush the glaze onto the cake. Brush or pour any glaze that drips onto the plate back onto the cake. Let the cake cool completely and serve at room temperature. For an extra touch of sweetness, sift confectioners' sugar over the cooled cake just before serving.

Sweet Potato–Walnut Bread

Sweet potatoes and yams are popular nowadays, and often I'll see what are clearly yams listed as sweet potatoes on a menu. The truth is, they both taste great and have high nutritional value. Either one will work in this recipe, so choose the one you like best. Just like when preparing carrots for making carrot cake, you want the sweet potatoes or yams finely shredded. The shredding disk on a food processor makes quick work of this task. This bread, wrapped in plastic wrap or slipped into an airtight tin and stored at room temperature, stays remarkably moist for 5 to 6 days. **MAKES 2 LOAVES**

2 cups unbleached all-purpose flour

1½ teaspoons baking powder

2 teaspoons baking soda

1 teaspoon salt

1 tablespoon ground ginger

2 teaspoons ground cinnamon

1 teaspoon ground cardamom, preferably freshly ground

¼ teaspoon freshly ground pepper

4 eggs, at room temperature

⅔ cup granulated sugar

⅔ cup firmly packed dark brown sugar

1¼ cups canola or other neutral-flavored vegetable oil

3 cups peeled and finely shredded sweet potato or yam (see headnote)

Grated zest and juice of 1 orange

1½ cups walnuts, chopped

1. Position a rack in the center of the oven and preheat to 350°F. Butter and flour two 8½-by-4½-by-2½-inch loaf pans.

2. In a large bowl, whisk together the flour, baking powder, baking soda, salt, ginger, cinnamon, cardamom, and pepper. In a large bowl, using a stand mixer fitted with the whip attachment or a handheld mixer, beat the eggs on medium speed until they have noticeably increased in volume, about 2 minutes. Slowly add the granulated and brown sugars and then the oil to the eggs and continue to beat until a thick, foamy mixture forms.

3. Using a wooden spoon, stir the egg mixture into the flour mixture until combined. Stir in the sweet potato, orange zest and juice, and the walnuts, mixing well. Divide the batter evenly between the prepared pans and smooth the tops.

4. Bake until the tops spring back when pressed lightly with a fingertip, 50 to 60 minutes. Let cool in the pans on wire racks for about 20 minutes. Run a knife around the inside edge of each pan to loosen the cake sides, then unmold the cakes onto the racks. Serve at room temperature.

NOTE: I like to bake this batter in mini loaf pans for giving as gifts. I use five 5-inch-long pans and bake the breads for 25 to 28 minutes. The sizes of mini loaf pans vary, so adjust the baking time accordingly.

Apricot-Blueberry Snack Cake

This cake is quick—no mixer required—and keeps for days tightly wrapped in plastic wrap and stored at room temperature. It is also a great way to showcase agave syrup, a minimally processed sweetener made from the agave cactus. If you cannot find blueberries, raspberries or blackberries also work well. If you use frozen berries, do not thaw them before adding them to the batter. To make this a sugar-free cake, seek out a no-sugar-sweetened peach or apricot fruit spread for glazing the berries. **MAKES ABOUT 9 SERVINGS**

1¼ cups unbleached all-purpose flour, sifted

1 teaspoon baking soda

½ teaspoon baking powder

¼ teaspoon ground cinnamon

¼ teaspoon salt

1 egg

⅔ cup agave syrup, preferably light, or ½ cup light-colored honey

5 tablespoons unsalted butter, melted

1 tablespoon grated orange zest

¼ cup boiling water

1 cup fresh or frozen blueberries

⅔ cup peach or apricot preserves or no-sugar-added fruit spread

1. Position a rack in the center of the oven and preheat to 350°F. Butter and flour an 8-inch square baking pan or spray with nonstick cooking spray.

2. In a medium bowl, whisk together the flour, baking soda, baking powder, cinnamon, and salt. In a large bowl, whisk the egg for about 2 minutes. Make sure it is well blended. Add the agave syrup and butter to the egg and whisk until thoroughly combined. Gently whisk in the flour mixture, then the orange zest, and finally the boiling water. Using a wooden spoon, stir in ½ cup of the blueberries. Pour the batter into the prepared pan and smooth the top. Scatter the remaining ½ cup berries evenly over the surface.

3. Bake until a cake tester inserted into the center comes out clean, 28 to 32 minutes. Transfer to a wire rack to cool.

4. To glaze the cake, spoon the preserves onto the cake while it is still hot from the oven, and use the back of the spoon or a brush to spread it evenly over the top. (The heat of the cake will lightly melt the preserves.) Let the cake cool completely before serving.

Ginger-Date-Pecan Bundt Cake

Dates were ubiquitous in the early days of the health food movement, used in everything from cakes to milk shakes, and date bars were everyday fare in the health food restaurants where I worked during my college days. For this recipe, I have kicked the date bar up a few notches to create a fitting tribute to this ancient fruit, one that allows its natural sweetness to be the main attraction. **MAKES 10 TO 12 SERVINGS**

2½ cups unbleached all-purpose flour

¾ cup granulated sugar

1 teaspoon baking powder

1 teaspoon baking soda

1 teaspoon ground cinnamon

¾ teaspoon salt

½ teaspoon ground nutmeg

½ teaspoon ground cardamom, preferably freshly ground

¾ cup canola or other neutral-flavored vegetable oil

¼ cup unsulfured molasses

3 eggs, at room temperature

¾ cup boiling water

⅔ cup crystallized ginger, chopped

1¼ cups pecans, chopped

1 cup dates, pitted, chopped, and tossed with 2 to 3 tablespoons flour to prevent sticking

Confectioners' sugar for dusting (optional)

1. Position a rack in the lower third of the oven and preheat to 350°F. Butter and flour a 10- to 12-cup Bundt or fluted tube pan.

2. In a large bowl, whisk together the flour, granulated sugar, baking powder, baking soda, cinnamon, salt, nutmeg, and cardamom. Measure the oil in a large glass measuring cup, add the molasses, and then whisk in the eggs, mixing well. Make a well in the flour mixture and pour in the oil mixture. Whisk together the dry and wet ingredients, gradually adding the boiling water as you whisk. (Do not pour the boiling water directly onto the egg mixture, or the eggs may curdle.) Stir in the ginger, pecans, and dates. Spread the batter in the prepared pan, smoothing the top.

3. Bake until a cake tester inserted into the center comes out clean, 40 to 50 minutes. Let cool in the pan on a wire rack for about 20 minutes. Invert the pan onto the rack to unmold the cake, then lift off the pan. Let cool completely before serving. If you like, sift confectioners' sugar over the cake just before serving.

The United States is now home to some of the most remarkable bakeries anywhere on the globe. Don't let this intimidate you into thinking that you should not attempt yeast breads at home, however, because you definitely should. I am not including recipes that take days to prepare. Instead, what you will find here are recipes designed for the home baker in the everyday home kitchen—recipes that are simple but not simplified or dumbed down.

Some of these baked treats are featured at Sweet Bar Bakery. The Honey Wheat Crescent Rolls grew out of my love of homemade rolls, a holiday staple when I was a kid. (We never used dough from a can!) Chocolate, Fig, & Walnut Snails will get anyone to eat chocolate for breakfast, even me. Maple-Pecan Sticky Buns came from my desire to add something new to a popular morning bun, and maple syrup was how I did it. Directions for making your own puff pastry could take up half a chapter, so I've opted for frozen commercial puff pastry for two of the turnover recipes. Seek out an all-butter brand, such as Dufour, if possible. But I have also included a turnover that encloses juicy pineapple in gingerbread—one of my all-time favorite morning treats.

Yeast Breads & Puff Pastry

Cinnamon Swirl Bread

If you liked making cinnamon toast as a child, you will love this freshly baked bread swirled with veins of cinnamon. I suppose the nuts could be optional, but I find the slightly tannic and toasty crunch a wonderful counterpoint to the tender cinnamon-laced bread. Reheat leftover slices in a toaster oven to recapture that freshly baked taste. Don't attempt to use a standard two-slice toaster, as the slices are too gooey. **MAKES 2 LOAVES**

DOUGH

1½ tablespoons canola or other neutral-flavored oil

2 teaspoons honey

1 envelope active dry yeast (2¼ teaspoons)

1½ cups unbleached all-purpose flour

1½ cups bread flour

1½ teaspoons salt

FILLING

4 tablespoons unsalted butter

½ cup sugar

1 tablespoon ground cinnamon

1¼ cups chopped walnuts, pecans, or hazelnuts

1 cup raisins

1. To make the dough, in the large bowl of a stand mixer, combine 1¼ cups lukewarm water (100° to 110°F), the oil, and the honey. Sprinkle the yeast over the top, stir to dissolve, and then let stand until foamy, about 5 minutes. Add the flours and salt. Fit the mixer with the dough hook and mix on low speed for about 7 minutes. The dough should be soft and somewhat sticky yet firm to the touch. You may need to add very small amounts of flour to keep the dough from sticking as you knead. Alternatively, combine the ingredients as directed and stir with a wooden spoon until the mixture comes together in a rough mass. Turn out onto a floured work surface and knead until the dough is soft and somewhat sticky yet firm to the touch, 10 to 12 minutes, adding small amounts of flour as needed to prevent sticking. Form the dough into a ball.

2. Lightly oil a large bowl. Transfer the dough to the bowl, turn the dough to coat on all sides with the oil, and cover the bowl with a kitchen towel or plastic wrap. Let the dough rise in a warm, draft-free spot until doubled in volume, about 1½ hours. Punch down the dough, re-cover, and let rise for another 30 minutes.

3. To make the filling, in a heavy saucepan, combine the butter, sugar, and 3 tablespoons water and bring to a rolling boil over high heat. Whisk in the cinnamon and immediately remove the pan from

continued >

the heat. (If the mixture gets too thick or begins to harden, swirl in another tablespoon or two of water over low heat.) Add the nuts and raisins and mix well. Set aside to cool.

4. Oil two 8½-by-4½-by-2½-inch loaf pans. Divide the dough in half. Lightly flour a work surface and place half of the dough on it. Using your hands, pat the dough into a rectangle about 10½ by 8 inches and about ½ inch thick, with a long side facing you. Starting from the long side nearest you, spread half of the cooled nut mixture length-wise over two-thirds of the dough, leaving the remaining one-third of the dough across the top and about 1 inch on each side uncovered. Starting at the edge nearest you, roll up the dough firmly, stopping at about the two-thirds point. Fold the uncovered sides toward the center, then continue to roll the dough, jelly-roll style, into a cylinder. Pinch the seam together as tightly as you can. Place the roll, seam side down, in a prepared pan. Repeat with the remaining dough and nut filling and place in the second pan. Cover each pan with a kitchen towel or plastic wrap and let the dough rise in a warm spot for 40 minutes.

5. Position one rack in the center and a second rack in the lower third of the oven and preheat to 400°F. Place a pan of extremely hot tap water on the lower rack.

6. When the oven is ready, using a serrated knife, make 3 or 4 diago-nal slashes in the top of each loaf, spacing them evenly apart to allow for expansion. Bake until the loaves are golden and sound hollow when tapped on top, 30 to 40 minutes. Let the loaves cool in the pans on wire racks for about 15 minutes, then use a long metal spatula to ease the loaves out of the pans onto the rack. Let cool completely before serving. (The loaves can be stored in an airtight container at room temperature for up to 4 days. Or, you can slice them, tightly wrap the slices individually, and freeze for up to 2 weeks.)

Honey Wheat Crescent Rolls

This is my version of the crescent roll, a holiday table classic that is rarely made from scratch any more. The all-purpose flour keeps these rolls light, the whole-wheat flour lends a nutty taste, and the melted butter and honey lift them up into the clouds. Serve them with butter and your favorite jam or preserves or with one of my spreads (pages 136 to 140). This recipe makes a big batch, so you may end up with some extra rolls. Wrap them tightly and freeze for up to 2 weeks, then thaw at room temperature and reheat in a hot oven or toaster oven. **MAKES 32 ROLLS**

¾ cup whole milk

½ cup (1 stick) plus 2 table-spoons unsalted butter, melted

⅓ cup light-colored honey

¾ teaspoon salt

1 envelope active dry yeast (2¼ teaspoons)

3 eggs, lightly beaten

3½ cups unbleached all-purpose flour, sifted

1 cup whole-wheat flour, preferably stone-ground

1 egg beaten with 1 tablespoon water for glaze

1. In a small saucepan, heat the milk over medium heat just until bubbles appear at the edge of the pan. Pour into a large bowl and add ½ cup of the melted butter, the honey, and the salt. Stir to dissolve the honey and let cool to lukewarm, about 15 minutes.

2. In a small bowl, sprinkle the yeast over ¼ cup lukewarm water (100° to 110°F), stir to dissolve, and let stand until foamy, about 5 minutes. Add the eggs and yeast mixture to the lukewarm milk mixture and stir with a wooden spoon, mixing well. Gradually add the flours and stir until the dough pulls together in a rough mass.

3. Lightly flour a work surface and turn the dough out onto it. Knead until smooth and elastic, about 10 minutes, adding small amounts of flour as you go if the dough is too sticky. The dough is ready when you can knead it without it sticking to the work surface, even when no excess flour is visible on the surface. Form the dough into a ball.

4. Place the dough in a large, clean bowl and cover with a kitchen towel. Let the dough rise in a warm, draft-free spot until doubled in volume, about 1 hour.

continued >

5. Line 2 baking sheets with parchment paper or nonstick baking mats. Turn the dough out onto a lightly floured work surface and divide in half. Shape each half into a ball. Flatten one ball into a disk and then roll it out into a 12-inch circle. Brush the circle lightly with 1 tablespoon of the remaining melted butter. Cut the circle into 16 equal wedges. Starting from the wide, round end of each wedge, roll up the wedge to the pointed end. Arrange the rolls, pointed end down, on a prepared baking sheet, spacing them about 1½ inches apart. Curve them into a crescent shape by bringing the two ends toward each other. Repeat with the second half of the dough to make 16 more rolls, and arrange them on the second baking sheet. Brush the rolls with the egg glaze. Cover the baking sheets loosely with a kitchen towel or plastic wrap and let the rolls rise in a warm spot until they have almost doubled in volume, about 45 minutes. (Alternatively, pour about 6 cups boiling water into a shallow pan and place the pan on the bottom of a cold oven. Put the pans of rolls in the oven and leave the rolls until they have noticeably risen, 15 to 20 minutes, then remove the baking sheets and the pan of water and begin preheating the oven.)

6. When the rolls are about halfway through their second rise, position a rack in the upper third and a second rack in the lower third of the oven and preheat to 350°F. When the oven is ready, bake the rolls, switching the pans between the racks and rotating them back to front about halfway through baking, until they are golden and sound slightly hollow when tapped on top, 18 to 20 minutes. Serve warm.

Maple-Pecan Sticky Buns

Most sticky buns are made with caramelized sugar and butter, but I find maple syrup much more enticing. First, its aroma fills the house when the buns are in the oven, and then, of course, there is the taste. Let me say, simply, maple syrup and maple sugar work in harmony to make these sticky buns divine. The maple sugar and butter cling to the inner layers of each bun, and the syrup ensures a gooey, shiny glaze on the surface when the buns are inverted. **MAKES 9 BUNS**

DOUGH

1 cup whole milk

2 tablespoons maple syrup

4 tablespoons unsalted butter, cut into small pieces

1 envelope active dry yeast (2¼ teaspoons)

2½ cups unbleached all-purpose flour

½ teaspoon salt

GLAZE AND FILLING

½ cup (1 stick) unsalted butter, at room temperature, plus 1 tablespoon, melted

1 cup pecan halves or pieces

⅔ cup maple syrup

½ cup maple sugar

1 tablespoon ground cinnamon

1 cup raisins

1. To make the dough, in a medium saucepan, heat the milk over medium heat just until bubbles appear at the edge of the pan. Remove from the heat and stir in the maple syrup and butter. Let cool until lukewarm (100° to 110°F). Sprinkle in the yeast, stir to dissolve, and let stand until foamy, about 5 minutes.

2. In a large bowl, whisk together the flour and salt. Make a well in the flour mixture and pour in the milk mixture. Using a wooden spoon, stir together the dry and wet ingredients until a soft, sticky dough forms.

3. Lightly flour a work surface and turn the dough out onto the surface. Knead the dough until supple and elastic, about 8 minutes, adding small amounts of flour as you go if the dough is too sticky. Form the dough into a ball.

4. Butter a medium bowl. Transfer the dough to the bowl, turn the dough to coat on all sides with the butter, and cover the bowl with a kitchen towel. Let the dough rise in a warm, draft-free spot until doubled in volume and a finger pressed ½ inch into the dough leaves an impression, about 1 hour.

continued >

5. To make the glaze, butter a 9-inch square glass baking dish with 1 tablespoon of the room-temperature butter. Sprinkle the pecans evenly over the bottom. Pour the maple syrup evenly over the pecans. To make the filling, in a small bowl, stir together the maple sugar, cinnamon, and the remaining 7 tablespoons room-temperature butter until a spreadable paste forms. Set aside.

6. Punch down the dough and turn it out onto a lightly floured work surface. Roll out the dough into a 15-by-12-inch rectangle. With a long side of the dough facing you, drop the maple-butter mixture by spoonfuls onto the dough, spacing them evenly. Then, using an offset spatula, spread the mixture evenly over the dough, leaving a 1-inch border at the long side nearest you. Sprinkle the raisins evenly over the maple-butter mixture. Starting at the long side farthest from you, roll up the dough into a firm, thick cylinder. Using a sharp knife, cut the cylinder crosswise into 9 equal slices, each about 1¾ inches wide. Arrange the slices, with a cut side down, in the prepared baking dish.

7. Cover the baking dish with a kitchen towel or plastic wrap and place in a warm spot. Let the buns rise until they have almost doubled in volume, about 45 minutes. When the buns are about halfway through their rise, position a rack in the center of the oven and preheat to 375°F.

8. Brush the tops of the buns with the 1 tablespoon melted butter. Bake until the tops are browned and the sauce is bubbling in the center, 30 to 35 minutes. Remove from the oven and immediately invert the baking dish onto a serving platter. Scrape any nuts and syrup clinging to the bottom of the dish onto the buns. Let cool for about 20 minutes, then serve warm.

Chocolate, Fig & Walnut Snails

It is such a luxury to have chocolate at breakfast, so I wanted to make a recipe worthy of the indulgence. This is it. After considerable chocolate taste testing (I know, sometimes my work is tough!), I have come to the conclusion that bittersweet or semisweet chocolate and figs are a match made in heaven. It takes a bit of effort to work all the chocolate, dried fruit, and nuts into the dough, but taste testers have convinced me not to cut back. Think of the extra kneading as good exercise. **MAKES 12 SNAILS**

3 cups bread flour

¼ cup sugar

2 envelopes quick-rising yeast (2¼ teaspoons each)

1 teaspoon salt

½ cup buttermilk

2 eggs

2 tablespoons unsalted butter, melted

1 cup semisweet chocolate chips or bittersweet chocolate chunks

1½ cups dried figs, chopped

¾ cup coarsely chopped walnuts

1 egg beaten with 1 tablespoon water for glaze

1. In a large bowl, whisk together the flour, sugar, yeast, and salt. Add the buttermilk, eggs, and butter and stir vigorously with a wooden spoon until well blended. Gradually stir in about ⅓ cup hot water to form a soft, slightly sticky dough.

2. Lightly flour a work surface and turn the dough out onto it. Knead the dough until smooth and slightly tacky but not sticky, about 7 minutes, adding small amounts of flour as you go if the dough is too sticky. Knead in the chocolate chips and dried figs, ⅓ cup at a time, until evenly distributed. Then knead in the walnuts. The nuts are a bit difficult to work into the dough but are well worth the effort. Form the dough into a ball.

3. Oil a large bowl. Transfer the dough to the bowl, turn the dough to coat on all sides with the oil, and cover the bowl with plastic wrap and then a kitchen towel. Let the dough rise in a warm, draft-free spot until doubled in volume, about 1½ hours.

4. Lightly oil a large, heavy baking sheet. Lightly flour a work surface. Punch down the dough. A word of warning: This dough is a bit sticky from the chocolate and the warmth of rising. Flour it generously and then brush off the excess flour after you have shaped it. Turn the dough out onto the floured surface. Divide the dough into 4 equal portions, then divide each portion into 3 equal portions. You should

continued >

have 12 equal portions in all. Using your palms, and dusting them with flour if needed, roll one dough portion into a 13-inch-long rope. Starting in the center, curl the rope into concentric circles to form a snail shape. Tuck the ends under and pinch together. Transfer to the prepared baking sheet. Brush with some of the egg glaze. Repeat with the remaining dough portions, spacing them evenly apart on the baking sheet.

5. Let the snails rise, uncovered, in a warm spot until almost doubled in volume, about 1¼ hours. When the snails have risen for just under an hour, position a rack in the center of the oven and preheat to 325°F.

6. Brush the snails again with the egg glaze. Bake until they are deep golden brown and sound hollow when tapped on the bottom, about 18 minutes. Serve warm.

NOTE: The snails can be made in advance. Bake as directed and let cool completely on the pan on a wire rack. Wrap tightly in aluminum foil, place in a zip-top plastic bag, and freeze for up to 2 weeks. Unwrap and let thaw at room temperature, then sprinkle with a few drops of water and reheat in a hot oven or toaster oven.

Orange-Almond Honey Buns

On those mornings when you don't have time for yeast-leavened baking—the time to mix, knead, and rise—don't fret! These honey buns will fool people into thinking that you have been up since dawn. Thanks to the honey, they are moist, with a tender crumb and a nice shine. **MAKES 12 BUNS**

DOUGH

2 cups unbleached all-purpose flour

1 tablespoon baking powder

1 teaspoon salt

4 tablespoons cold unsalted butter, cut into small pieces

¾ cup buttermilk, or more if needed

FILLING

3 tablespoons unsalted butter, at room temperature

⅓ cup light-colored honey

1 teaspoon ground cinnamon

1 teaspoon ground cardamom, preferably freshly ground (optional)

Grated zest of 1 large orange

MUFFIN TIN

3 tablespoons unsalted butter

⅓ cup light-colored honey

½ cup sliced almonds

1. Position a rack in the center of the oven and preheat to 375°F. Have ready a 12-cup standard muffin tin.

2. To make the dough, in a medium bowl, sift together the flour, baking powder, and salt. Scatter the butter over the top. Using a pastry blender or your fingers, work in the butter until the mixture resembles coarse crumbs. Make a well in the flour mixture and pour in ¾ cup buttermilk. Stir with a wooden spoon until a soft but not sticky dough forms. Add more buttermilk, 1 tablespoon at a time, if the dough is too dry and will not pull together.

3. Lightly flour a work surface and turn the dough out onto it. Knead gently a few times and then gather it into a ball. Let the dough rest while you prepare the filling and the muffin tin.

4. To make the filling, whisk together the butter, honey, cinnamon, cardamom, and orange zest until a smooth paste forms. Set aside.

5. To prepare the muffin tin, divide the butter and honey evenly among the 12 muffin cups, putting about ¾ teaspoon butter and a scant 1½ teaspoons honey in each cup. The butter and honey will caramelize and stick to the buns during baking. Divide the almond slices evenly among the cups, pressing them lightly into the honey and butter.

continued >

6. Clean the work surface, then once again dust it lightly with flour. Transfer the dough to the surface and roll it out into a 15-by-10-inch rectangle about ¼ inch thick, lightly flouring the surface of the dough as necessary to prevent sticking and lifting the dough as needed to square off the edges and corners. Trim the edges to even them as needed, then brush off any excess flour. With a long side of the dough facing you, spread the filling evenly over the dough with an offset spatula, leaving a 1-inch border along the top. Starting at the long side nearest you, roll up the dough into a thick, firm cylinder, tucking it under with your fingers to tighten as you work your way to the opposite edge. Using a sharp knife, cut the cylinder crosswise into 12 equal slices, each about 1¼ inches wide. Place each slice, with a cut side down, in a prepared muffin cup.

7. Bake until the buns are nicely browned, about 18 minutes. Remove from the oven and immediately invert the muffin tin onto a large serving platter, scraping any topping clinging to the bottom of the tin onto the buns. Alternatively, loosen the edges of the buns with a knife and gently lift the buns onto a platter, scooping out and adding any topping left behind in the pan to the buns. Serve warm. These buns taste best when eaten the day they are baked.

Cinnamon-Ricotta Breakfast "Pretzels"

This recipe calls for a relatively small amount of yeast, so the dough rises only slightly and is pretzel-like. The ricotta tenderizes the dough, however, resulting in a texture that is soft and chewy, rather than crisp like a pretzel. Take the time to shape the dough into pretzel-style knots. If you goof up, you can unwind the dough—it is very forgiving—and try again! This is a great recipe to make with kids, and no matter what shapes end up on the baking sheet, these morning sweets, which are brushed with butter and tossed in cinnamon sugar when they are hot from the oven, will taste and look wonderful. **MAKES 12 PRETZELS**

DOUGH

3 cups bread flour

½ cup sugar

1 envelope quick-rising yeast (2¼ teaspoons)

1¼ teaspoons salt

½ cup whole-milk or part-skim ricotta cheese

3 eggs

4 tablespoons unsalted butter, melted

TOPPING

¼ cup sugar

2 teaspoons ground cinnamon

About 4 tablespoons unsalted butter, melted

1. To make the dough, in a large bowl, stir together the flour, sugar, yeast, and salt. Add the ricotta, eggs, and butter and stir vigorously until well blended. Gradually stir in about ⅓ cup hot water to form a soft, slightly sticky dough.

2. Lightly flour a work surface and turn the dough out onto it. Knead the dough until smooth and slightly tacky but not sticky, about 7 minutes, adding small amounts of flour as you go if the dough is too sticky. Form the dough into a ball.

3. Oil a large bowl. Transfer the dough to the bowl, turn the dough to coat on all sides with the oil, and cover the bowl with plastic wrap and then a kitchen towel. Let the dough rise in a warm, draft-free spot until doubled in volume, about 1½ hours.

4. Lightly brush 2 large, heavy baking sheets with oil. Punch down the dough. Turn the dough out onto an unfloured work surface. Divide the dough into 4 equal portions, then divide each portion into 3 equal portions. You should have 12 equal portions in all. Using your palms, roll each dough portion into an 8-inch-long rope. Let the dough rest for a few minutes, then stretch and roll each rope until it is 13 to 14 inches long. Working with 1 rope at a time, pull the two ends of the rope toward you, fold one end over the other about two-thirds of the

continued >

way down, and then give the ends a twist so they are crossed. Gently pull the rounded center of the rope outward to form a circle. Bring the twisted ends up to rest on the top edge of the circle. Press the ends firmly into the dough to secure. Transfer the pretzel to a prepared baking sheet. Repeat with remaining dough ropes, spacing the pretzels evenly apart on the baking sheets.

5. Let the pretzels rise, uncovered, in a warm spot until almost doubled in volume, about 45 minutes. When the pretzels are about halfway through their rise, position one rack in the lower third and a second rack in the upper third of the oven and preheat to 325°F.

6. Bake the pretzels, switching the pans between the racks and rotating them back to front about halfway through baking, until they are deep golden brown and sound hollow when tapped on the bottom, about 20 minutes. Transfer to a wire rack and let cool briefly. While the pretzels are cooling, make the topping. Stir together the cinnamon and sugar in a bowl wide enough to accommodate a pretzel.

7. Brush the still-warm pretzels on all sides with the butter and toss them in the cinnamon sugar. Serve warm. The pretzels taste best when eaten the day they are baked, but they can be stored in an airtight container at room temperature for a day or so and then reheated in a moderate oven or a toaster oven.

Strawberry-Rhubarb Turnovers

These turnovers are perfect for springtime and early summer, when rhubarb and strawberries have just come into the market. Be sure the sweet, ripe fruit for the filling is cut into slices, not chunks, or the pieces will poke through the pastry. **MAKES 12 TURNOVERS**

½ cup plus 2 tablespoons sugar

2 tablespoons cornstarch

3 cups sliced rhubarb (¼- to ⅓-inch-wide slices)

1 cup sliced strawberries (about ⅓-inch-thick slices)

2 frozen puff pastry sheets (from one 17¼-ounce package), thawed according to package directions

1 egg, lightly beaten

1. Position a rack in the center of the oven and preheat to 425°F. Line two baking sheets with parchment paper or nonstick baking mats for easy cleanup or brush with melted butter.

2. In a small bowl, whisk together the ½ cup sugar and the cornstarch. In a medium bowl, combine the rhubarb and strawberries and stir to mix.

3. Lightly flour a work surface and place a puff pastry sheet on it. Roll out the pastry into a 12- by-9-inch rectangle. Cut into 6 roughly 4-inch squares. Divide half of the fruit mixture evenly among the squares, leaving a 1-inch border on all sides. Lightly brush the border on each square with egg. Dot the filling on each square with 2 heaping teaspoons of the cornstarch mixture. Fold each pastry square into a triangle, enclosing the filling, and crimp the edges with a fork. Cut 2 small steam vents in the top of each triangle. Place the turnovers on a prepared baking sheet. Brush the tops with egg, then sprinkle each turnover with about ½ teaspoon sugar.

4. Bake until the turnovers are puffed, golden brown, and the fruit filling is bubbling in the steam vents, 18 to 20 minutes. Immediately transfer the turnovers to a wire rack to cool briefly.

5. While the first 6 turnovers are in the oven, make 6 more turnovers with the remaining pastry sheet, fruit filling, and cornstarch mixture. Place them on the second baking sheet, brush them with egg, and sprinkle with the remaining sugar. When the first batch of turnovers comes out of the oven, bake the second batch. Serve the turnovers warm.

Fig & Gorgonzola Turnovers

While working on the recipes that would open Sweet Bar Bakery, I noted that a significant number of people asked if there would be savory baked goods. Not all people have a sweet tooth, and I wanted to satisfy everyone's cravings! Cheese is one of the best ways to infuse savory baked goods with flavor, and Gorgonzola is at the top of the cheese list. Cheddar cheese and apples are another good filling for this recipe. **MAKES 12 TURNOVERS**

2 frozen puff pastry sheets (from one 17¼-ounce package), thawed according to package directions

2 cups stemmed and sliced fresh figs

About 1 cup (4 ounces) crumbled Gorgonzola or other blue cheese

1 egg, lightly beaten

1. Position a rack in the center of the oven and preheat to 425°F. Line 2 baking sheets with parchment paper or nonstick baking mats for easy cleanup or brush with butter.

2. Lightly flour a work surface and place a pastry sheet on it. Roll out the pastry into a 12- by-9-inch rectangle. Cut into 6 roughly 4-inch squares. Divide half of the figs and half of the Gorgonzola evenly among the squares, leaving a 1-inch border on all sides. Lightly brush the border of one square with egg, then fold each corner of the square into the center, enclosing the filling, and press down where the edges overlap to seal. Repeat with the remaining squares. Place the turnovers on a prepared baking sheet and brush the tops with egg.

3. Bake until the turnovers are puffed and golden brown, 18 to 20 minutes. Immediately transfer the turnovers to a wire rack.

4. While the first 6 turnovers are in the oven, make 6 more turnovers with the remaining pastry sheet, figs, and Gorgonzola. Place the turnovers on the second prepared baking sheet and brush with egg. When the first batch of turnovers comes out of the oven, place the second batch in the oven and bake as directed. Serve the turnovers warm or at room temperature.

Pineapple-Gingerbread Turnovers

If you are tempted to make these turnovers with canned pineapple, resist the urge. Because pineapples are grown in Hawaii and flown to markets all over the United States, you can have a true taste of the tropics with this recipe. Find out where to buy the freshest and tastiest pineapples in your area and how to tell when they are ripe. You may want to seek out Hawaiian ginger, too. This recipe is worth it! **MAKES 8 TURNOVERS**

DOUGH

2½ cups unbleached all-purpose flour

2 teaspoons baking powder

½ teaspoon salt

½ cup (1 stick) unsalted butter, at room temperature

½ cup firmly packed light brown sugar

3 eggs

1 teaspoon vanilla extract

2 tablespoons peeled and grated fresh ginger (use the smallest holes of a box grater)

1. Make the dough at least 2 hours before you plan to bake the turnovers. In a medium bowl, whisk together the flour, baking powder, and salt. In a large bowl, using a stand mixer, fitted with the paddle attachment, cream together the butter and brown sugar on medium speed until light in color and texture, about 3 minutes. Add the eggs, one at a time, and beat well after each addition. Add the vanilla and ginger and beat until combined. On low speed, add the flour mixture and beat until thoroughly combined. (Alternatively, use a large bowl and a handheld mixer for beating the wet ingredients, then stir in the flour mixture with a wooden spoon.)

2. Gather up the dough and divide it in half. Flatten each half into a thick disk. Wrap each disk in plastic wrap and refrigerate until chilled and firm, at least 2 hours or up to overnight.

3. Position a rack in the center of the oven and preheat to 400°F. Line 2 baking sheets with parchment paper or nonstick baking mats.

4. To make the filling, in a small bowl, whisk together the brown sugar, flour, and lemon zest. Chop the pineapple into ½-inch dice. You should have 2 cups. In a medium bowl, mix half of the flour mixture with half of the pineapple. (To discourage the pineapple from giving off too much juice, chop it just before you make the filling, and mix the pineapple with the flour mixture in two batches.)

FILLING

⅓ cup firmly packed light
brown sugar

1 tablespoon unbleached
all-purpose flour

Grated zest of 1 lemon

About ¼ large pineapple,
peeled and cored

1 egg beaten with 2 teaspoons
water for glaze

Granulated sugar for sprinkling

5. Lightly flour a work surface and place a dough disk on it. Roll out the dough into a 12-inch square. Cut into four 6-inch squares. Place one-fourth of the pineapple-flour mixture in the center of a square and lightly brush the border of the square with the egg glaze. Fold the square into a triangle, enclosing the filling, and press the edges gently but firmly. Dip the tines of a fork in flour, then press the edges with the fork tines to seal. Place the turnover on a prepared baking sheet and poke air holes in the top with the fork tines. Fill the remaining 3 squares the same way, add to the baking sheet, and pierce the tops. (Do not make the turnovers until you are ready to bake them, as the pineapple quickly gives off its juices.) Brush the turnovers with some of the egg glaze and sprinkle with granulated sugar.

6. Bake until the turnovers are golden brown, 15 to 18 minutes. Transfer to a wire rack to cool.

7. While the first 4 turnovers are in the oven, mix together the remaining pineapple and flour mixture and use to make 4 more turnovers with the remaining dough disk. Place the turnovers on the second prepared baking sheet, brush with the egg glaze, and sprinkle with granulated sugar. When the first batch of turnovers comes out of the oven, place the second batch in the oven and bake as directed. Serve the turnovers warm or at room temperature.

In the United States, biscuits are a national tradition, and scones are viewed as somewhat exotic. But American biscuits and Scottish scones are often made the same way: you work butter into flour until it is evenly distributed but still in relatively large chunks, add liquid to form a dough, knead the dough briefly, cut it into shapes, and bake. The results are similar, too: tender-crumbed, buttery, flaky small "breads" that nearly everyone seems to love. To ensure success when making them, don't overwork the dough (you are not kneading bread!), leave the butter in chunks that are bigger than you might think they should be, and gently stir in any additions, such as berries or dried fruits. Once all of the ingredients are combined, the dough will begin to "pull together," as the flour slowly absorbs the wet ingredients.

Both biscuits and scones benefit from a slightly dry interior, which allows the butter to impart flavor and texture. The best way to add moisture is to serve them with plenty of honey butter, preserves, or other spreads. See pages 136 to 140 for an array of accompaniments that you can make yourself.

Scones and biscuits are always best when eaten fresh from the oven, but you can slip any leftovers into an airtight container or zip-top plastic bag and store them at room temperature for a day or two. Reheat them in a moderate oven or toaster oven before serving.

Scones
&
Biscuits

Pumpkin Biscuits

That little bit of extra pumpkin remaining after making pie and other goodies, such as my Pumpkin-Cranberry Tea Cake (page 42), is all the excuse you need to whip up a batch of these biscuits just in time for your next breakfast. Serve with liberal amounts of Orange Honey Butter (page 139). **MAKES 15 TO 18 BISCUITS**

3 cups unbleached all-purpose flour

⅓ cup firmly packed brown sugar

4 teaspoons baking powder

¾ teaspoon salt

½ teaspoon ground cinnamon

½ cup (1 stick) cold unsalted butter, cut into small pieces

1 cup plus 2 tablespoons half-and-half

¾ cup pumpkin puree

1. Position a rack in the center of the oven and preheat to 425°F. Line a baking sheet with parchment paper or a nonstick baking mat.

2. In a medium bowl, whisk together the flour, brown sugar, baking powder, salt, and cinnamon. Scatter the butter over the flour mixture. Using a pastry blender or your fingers, work in the butter until the mixture resembles large, coarse crumbs. Make a well in the flour mixture and pour in the 1 cup half-and-half and the pumpkin. Using a wooden spoon or a plastic dough scraper, fold the ingredients together just until the dough pulls together.

3. Lightly flour a work surface and turn the dough out onto it. Knead the dough until it forms a workable ball, ten or twelve turns, then pat into a round about ¾ inch thick. Using a 2- to 2½-inch biscuit cutter or the rim of a water glass, cut out as many rounds as possible, dipping the cutter in flour before each cut. Place the rounds on the prepared baking sheet, spacing them about 1 inch apart. Gather up the dough scraps, gently knead them together, pat out the dough ¾ inch thick, and cut out more rounds. Add them to the baking sheet. Brush the tops of the biscuits with the 2 tablespoons half-and-half.

4. Bake until the biscuits are lightly browned, 13 to 15 minutes. Let cool on the pan on a wire rack for a few minutes, then serve warm.

Classic Currant Scones

These all-around scones are versatile enough to smear with butter at breakfast or to pair with jam and cream at teatime, British style, yet tasty all on their own. There are two keys to their success: Be sure the butter is still visible in pea-sized chunks when you are mixing the dough, and use a high-quality large-grain sugar (but not too much!). I was taught by a baker whose name escapes me that the butter for scones should be in chunks "bigger than you think. Remember, this is not a pie dough that has to be elastic enough to roll, so you don't want to overwork the butter." Because the British Isles and particularly Scotland are so closely connected with scones, it is fitting to use the type of sugar most commonly used there, which is Demerara or turbinado, not the moist brown sugar used in the States. **MAKES 8 SCONES**

1½ cups unbleached all-purpose
    flour

6 tablespoons Demerara or
    turbinado sugar

¾ cup old-fashioned rolled oats

2 teaspoons baking powder

½ teaspoon salt

6 tablespoons cold unsalted
    butter, cut into ¼-inch dice

½ cup buttermilk, plus more
    for glazing

½ cup dried currants

1. Position a rack in the center of the oven and preheat to 425°F. Line a baking sheet with parchment paper or a nonstick baking mat.

2. In a large bowl, whisk together the flour, 3 tablespoons of the Demerara sugar, the rolled oats, the baking powder, and the salt. Scatter the butter over the flour mixture. Using a pastry blender or your fingers, work in the butter until the mixture resembles large, coarse crumbs. Make a well in the flour mixture, pour in the ½ cup buttermilk and the currants, and stir just until the dough comes together. It will look rough. Knead the dough a few times in the bowl to smooth it out a little. Do not overwork it.

3. Lightly flour a work surface and turn the dough out onto it. Knead the dough until it forms a workable ball, three or four turns, then pat into a round about 8½ inches in diameter and ¾ inch thick. Using a sharp knife, cut into 8 equal wedges. Lightly brush the tops with a little buttermilk and sprinkle with the remaining 3 tablespoons Demerara sugar. Gently lift each scone onto the prepared baking sheet, spacing them about 1 inch apart.

4. Bake until the scones are golden brown, 15 to 18 minutes. Let cool on the pan on a wire rack for a few minutes, then serve warm.

Strawberry Buttermilk Scones

Most of the scones served in the United States are not as rich and buttery as their British Isles origins would dictate. In fact, they tend to resemble a muffin. I've taken the best of both traditions to create a moist yet crisp scone: golden brown, packed with berries, with a dollop of preserves in the center. Strawberries tend to shrivel in the oven due to their high water content, so you'll want to begin with nice chunks. I recommend cutting them into quarters rather than slices. If the berries are large, cut them into sixths and measure them after they are cut. **MAKES 12 SCONES**

1¾ cups plus 2 tablespoons unbleached all-purpose flour

⅓ cup sugar

1½ teaspoons baking powder

½ teaspoon baking soda

¼ teaspoon salt

4 tablespoons cold unsalted butter, cut into small pieces

1 egg, lightly beaten

1 cup buttermilk

1½ cups fresh or frozen strawberries, hulled and quartered

GARNISH

About ¼ cup strawberry jam or preserves

2 tablespoons sugar

1. Position a rack in the center of the oven and preheat to 425°F. Line a baking sheet with parchment paper or a nonstick baking mat.

2. In a large bowl, whisk together the flour, sugar, baking powder, baking soda, and salt. Scatter the butter over the flour mixture. Using a pastry blender or your fingers, work in the butter until the mixture resembles large, coarse crumbs. Make a well in the flour mixture and pour in the egg and buttermilk. Using a wooden spoon, turn and cut through the mixture until it starts to come together in a shaggy dough. Add the berries and continue to turn and cut through the mixture until it comes together in a slightly sticky ball, adding small amounts of flour as you go if the dough is too sticky to handle. Do not try to knead the dough.

3. Using an ice cream scoop or a large spoon, scoop the dough onto the prepared baking sheet, making 12 equal-sized mounds in all and spacing them at least 1½ inches apart. To garnish each scone, lightly press a thumb-sized indentation into the center of the mound and drop a generous rounded teaspoon of the jam into the indentation. Sprinkle the dough around the jam with the sugar, dividing it evenly among the scones.

4. Bake until the scones are golden brown, about 18 minutes. Let cool on the pan on a wire rack for a few minutes, then serve warm.

Savory Rosemary-Semolina Scones

Here is a scone recipe for anyone who likes something freshly baked in the morning but who, like me, doesn't always want something sweet. The olive oil, chèvre, and honey meld together wonderfully. Butter would not work here because it would overpower the subtlety of the other ingredients. If you like, serve with additional chèvre and honey. **MAKES 8 TO 10 SCONES**

1⅓ cups unbleached all-purpose flour

1⅓ cups semolina

2 teaspoons baking powder

½ teaspoon baking soda

½ teaspoon salt

4 tablespoons olive oil

1½ teaspoons finely chopped fresh rosemary

¼ cup mild-flavored herbal honey such as lavender, sage, or eucalyptus

1 egg

½ cup heavy cream or whole milk, plus more for glazing

5 ounces chèvre (semisoft goat cheese)

1. Position a rack in the center of the oven and preheat to 425°F. Line a baking sheet with parchment paper or a nonstick baking mat.

2. In a medium bowl, sift together the flour, semolina, baking powder, baking soda, and salt. In a second medium bowl, stir together lightly the oil, 1 teaspoon of the rosemary, the honey, the egg, and ½ cup cream. Whisk just enough to break up the egg yolk and blend the honey.

3. Add the goat cheese to the flour mixture and, using a pastry blender or your fingers, work in the cheese until the mixture resembles large, coarse crumbs (use the same technique you use for cutting butter into flour). Make a well in the flour mixture and pour in the oil mixture. Using a wooden spoon, stir together the dry and wet ingredients just until the mixture comes together in a ball. Knead the dough gently in the bowl several times.

4. Lightly flour a work surface and turn the dough out onto it. Knead again a few turns, just enough to make a workable ball. Pat the dough into a round about 8½ inches in diameter and ¾ inch thick. The edges may crack; use your palm to shape and repair the cracks. (The semolina makes the dough somewhat less cohesive than a dough made with only all-purpose flour.) Using a sharp knife, cut the round into 8 or 10 equal wedges. Lightly brush the tops with cream and sprinkle evenly with the remaining ½ teaspoon rosemary. Gently lift the scones onto the prepared baking sheet, spacing them about 1 inch apart.

5. Bake until the scones are golden brown, 12 to 15 minutes. Let cool briefly on a wire rack, then serve warm.

Chocolate-Blackberry Scones

One day while visiting Northern California's wine country, I got to thinking: how can I capture the experience of a bold wine in a simple breakfast baking format? The flavor descriptions that came to mind to describe the full-bodied red wines I like included jammy, berries, hints of cocoa, chocolatey . . . and there it was: blackberries and a few good-sized chunks of chocolate. I combined them in this tasty, rustic scone. It doesn't call for much sugar, so the berries and chocolate really pop. Chocolate chips will work, but I encourage you to chop up a really good bar of your favorite bittersweet chocolate. You'll need just 4 to 6 large chunks per scone to capture the balance of flavors here. **MAKES 9 SCONES**

1 cup whole-wheat flour

1 cup unbleached all-purpose flour

8 tablespoons sugar

1 tablespoon baking powder

½ teaspoon salt

4 tablespoons cold unsalted butter, cut into small pieces

¾ cup whole-milk or low-fat plain yogurt

1 egg, lightly beaten

½ cup (about 3 ounces) bitter-sweet chocolate chunks

1½ cups fresh or frozen blackberries

1. Position a rack in the center of the oven and preheat to 425°F. Line a baking sheet with parchment paper or a nonstick baking mat.

2. In a large bowl, whisk together the flours, 5 tablespoons of the sugar, the baking powder, and the salt. Scatter the butter over the flour mixture. Using a pastry blender or your fingers, work in the butter until the mixture resembles large, coarse crumbs. Make a well in the flour mixture and pour in the yogurt, egg, chocolate chunks, and berries. Using a wooden spoon, stir just until the dough comes together. It will look rough.

3. Using a large spoon, drop the dough onto the prepared baking sheet in 9 equal-sized mounds, spacing them at least 1½ inches apart. (This dough is denser than most scone doughs and can easily be "dropped," though you can scoop it as well.) Sprinkle each mound with 1 teaspoon of the remaining sugar.

4. Bake until the scones are golden brown, 15 to 18 minutes. Let cool on the pan on a wire rack for a few minutes, then serve warm.

Banana Scones

This is a sticky dough that makes an American-style scone, like a muffin top, loaded with chunks of banana and perfumed with nutmeg and vanilla. Served fresh or toasted the next day, these scones are a great way to enjoy such spreads as Strawberry-Rhubarb Preserves (page 140) or Lemon Mascarpone Cream (page 139). Gently folding and turning the dough instead of kneading it saves a few steps and helps retain the moist banana flavor. **MAKES 12 TO 15 SCONES**

2¾ cups unbleached all-purpose flour, plus more for mixing

½ cup plus 2 tablespoons sugar

4 teaspoons baking powder

½ teaspoon ground cinnamon

½ teaspoon ground nutmeg

½ teaspoon salt

6 tablespoons cold unsalted butter, cut into small pieces

½ cup plus 3 tablespoons buttermilk

1 egg, lightly beaten

1 teaspoon vanilla extract

2 cups ½-inch chunks bananas (about 3 large, ripe bananas)

1. Position a rack in the center of the oven and preheat to 425°F. Line a baking sheet with parchment paper or a nonstick baking sheet.

2. In a medium bowl, whisk together the 2¾ cups flour, the ½ cup sugar, the baking powder, cinnamon, nutmeg, and salt. Scatter the butter over the flour mixture. Using a pastry blender or your fingers, work in the butter until the mixture resembles large, coarse crumbs. Make a well in the flour mixture and pour in the ½ cup buttermilk, the egg, and vanilla. Using a wooden spoon, lightly stir and fold together the dry and wet ingredients until the dry ingredients are almost absorbed. Add the banana and fold the ingredients together with the wooden spoon or a plastic dough scraper. Sprinkle a little additional flour over the dough, turn the dough a few times in the bowl, and let sit for about 20 minutes.

3. Using an ice cream scoop or a large spoon, scoop the dough onto the prepared baking sheet, forming 12 to 15 equal-sized mounds and spacing them at least 1½ inches apart. Brush the tops with the 3 tablespoons buttermilk and sprinkle evenly with the 2 tablespoons sugar.

4. Bake until the scones are lightly browned, about 20 minutes. Let cool on the pan on a wire rack for a few minutes, then serve warm.

Whole-Grain Drop Biscuits

Whole-wheat pastry flour is a low-protein flour with less gluten than all-purpose flour, making it the perfect choice for tender whole-grain baked goods. Do not substitute standard whole-wheat flour or the biscuits will be tough. These are drop biscuits, so no kneading is required. They are a great way to showcase jams and preserves and pair well with eggs prepared any style and with egg dishes such as frittatas and omelets.

MAKES ABOUT 18 BISCUITS

2 cups whole-wheat pastry flour

1 tablespoon sugar

4 teaspoons baking powder

1 teaspoon baking soda

½ teaspoon salt

5 tablespoons cold unsalted butter, cut into small pieces

1⅓ cups whole-milk plain yogurt

1 egg

SAVORY OPTION

1 cup bite-sized chunks Gruyère or Parmesan cheese (see note)

4 slices bacon, fried until crisp and broken into ½-inch pieces

1½ teaspoons minced fresh rosemary

1. Position one rack in the upper third and a second rack in the lower third of the oven and preheat to 450°F. Line 2 baking sheets with parchment paper or nonstick baking mats.

2. In a medium bowl, whisk together the flour, sugar, baking powder, baking soda, and salt. Scatter the butter over the flour mixture. Using a pastry blender or your fingers, work in the butter until the mixture resembles large, coarse crumbs. Do not overmix. Pea-sized chunks of butter should be visible.

3. In a small bowl, whisk together the yogurt and egg until well blended. Make a well in the flour mixture and pour in the yogurt mixture. If you want to make savory biscuits, add the cheese, bacon, and rosemary as well. Using a wooden spoon, stir just until the dough comes together. It will look rough. Drop the dough by the spoonful onto the prepared baking sheets, forming about 18 equal-sized mounds and spacing them evenly apart.

4. Bake the biscuits, switching the pans between the racks and rotating them back to front about halfway through baking, until browned (they will be quite dark because of the whole-wheat flour), 12 to 14 minutes. Let cool on the pans on wire racks for a few minutes, then serve.

NOTE: The flavor of cheese tends to diminish in the heat of the oven, so I like to cut it into small chunks for bigger bursts of cheese flavor. If you prefer, however, you can grate the cheese.

Blue Cheese Biscuits

The inclusion of cheese is a very European approach to the first meal of the day. Savory dishes and cheese as a protein source at breakfast are gaining traction here in the United States as well. These biscuits are a good choice when you want to offer both sweet and savory to round out a brunch menu. You need flour milled from high-protein hard wheat for this recipe, such as bread flour or pizza flour. **MAKES ABOUT 18 BISCUITS**

3 cups bread flour

4 teaspoons baking powder

1 teaspoon salt

½ cup (1 stick) cold unsalted butter, cut into small pieces

2 eggs

1 cup buttermilk

3 tablespoons light-colored honey

2 tablespoons olive oil

1½ cups crumbled blue cheese, plus 3 to 4 tablespoons for topping

¼ cup chopped green onions, white and tender green parts

1 egg beaten with 2 teaspoons water for glaze (optional)

¼ cup chopped nuts or whole seeds such as pecans or pumpkin seeds (optional)

1. Position one rack in the upper third and a second rack in the lower third of the oven and preheat to 400°F. Line 2 baking sheets with parchment paper or nonstick baking mats.

2. In a large bowl, whisk together the flour, baking powder, and salt. Scatter the butter over the flour mixture. Using a pastry blender or your fingers, work in the butter until the mixture resembles large, coarse crumbs.

3. In a small bowl, whisk together the eggs, buttermilk, honey, and oil until blended. Make a well in the flour mixture and pour in the egg mixture. Using a wooden spoon, stir and fold together the dry and wet ingredients until the dry ingredients are almost absorbed. Add the 1½ cups cheese and the green onions and continue to stir just until the dough comes together completely.

4. Flour a work surface liberally and turn the dough out onto it. Using your palms, pat out the dough about 1 inch thick. Fold half of the dough over onto itself, flatten the dough again to 1 inch thick, and repeat the folding. Repeat the flattening and folding two or three more times. The dough should now be smooth enough to press or roll out.

5. Roll or press out the dough ⅝ inch thick. Using a 2½-inch biscuit cutter or the rim of a water glass, cut out as many rounds as possible, dipping the cutter in flour before each cut. Place the rounds on the prepared baking sheets, putting no more than 9 rounds on each sheet and spacing the rounds evenly apart. Gather up the dough scraps, gently knead them together, pat out the dough ⅝ inch thick, and cut out more rounds. Add them to the baking sheet. If you want the biscuits to have a shiny appearance after baking, brush them with the egg glaze. Divide the 3 to 4 tablespoons cheese for topping and the nuts (if using) evenly among the tops of the rounds, pressing them gently so they adhere to the dough.

6. Bake the biscuits, switching the pans between the racks and rotating them back to front about halfway through baking, until golden brown, about 15 minutes. Let cool on the pans on wire racks for a few minutes, then serve.

One of the most popular breakfast foods in the United States, muffins are so widely available that I knew I couldn't just contribute another random array of blueberry, banana, and chocolate chip versions. The muffins here had to have a good reason to be included, something special that made them stand out from the crowd. For example, the Lemon-Ricotta Muffins tasted wonderful on their own. But the dollop of jam on top baked right into the batter, like a black bottom cupcake, and made the difference I was looking for. The two upside-down muffins, pineapple and banana, are good examples of taking a few simple extra steps to make the merely good into something truly memorable.

Muffins are great vehicles for getting whole grains into your diet, and I have included them in over half of the recipes in this chapter. The taste and texture of whole grains add to the enjoyment of eating muffins, whereas they might overpower a layer cake or other delicate baked item. Plus, muffins rich in whole grains are a savvy way to boost your nutrition intake at the start of the day.

Recipes for muffins almost shout out for variations. Try a different berry or fruit, add a streusel topping for extra decadence, or toss in some flax-seeds or flaxseed meal to up the fiber content. These are muffin recipes you can truly make your own.

Muffins

Brazilian Banana Upside-Down Muffins

We make a lot of upside-down muffins at Sweet Bar Bakery, and I think I know why they are so popular. Anyone can cut up fruit and toss it into a batter, and the resulting muffins will taste great. But if you take the time to layer the ingredients in the pan, caramelizing the fruit and sugar with a thin sheen of butter, a good muffin becomes a great muffin. It's well worth the extra effort. A Brazilian upside-down cake recipe was reworked to come up with these crowd-pleasing muffins. Freshly grate whole nutmeg for the best flavor, and seek out small bananas, such as the Manzano variety or those labeled "finger," for the creamiest taste.

MAKES 12 MUFFINS

TOPPING

6 tablespoons unsalted butter

½ cup firmly packed dark brown sugar

4 small, ripe bananas

MUFFINS

1 cup unbleached all-purpose flour

2 teaspoons baking powder

½ teaspoon ground nutmeg

¼ teaspoon salt

½ cup firmly packed dark brown sugar

⅓ cup canola or other neutral-flavored vegetable oil

2 eggs, at room temperature

3 tablespoons whole milk

3 tablespoons dark rum

1 teaspoon vanilla extract

1. Position a rack in the center of the oven and preheat to 375°F. Lightly brush a 12-cup standard muffin tin with melted butter.

2. To make the topping, add ½ tablespoon butter and 2 teaspoons brown sugar to each prepared muffin cup. Bake until the mixture in each cup is melted and bubbly, about 10 minutes. Remove from the oven and let cool for a few minutes. Peel the bananas and cut each on the diagonal into 12 thin slices. Place 2 banana slices on the bottom and 2 banana slices along the sides of each muffin cup.

3. To make the muffins, in a large bowl, sift together the flour, baking powder, nutmeg, and salt. In a medium bowl, whisk together the brown sugar, oil, eggs, milk, rum, and vanilla. Make a well in the flour mixture and pour in the sugar mixture. Using a wooden spoon, stir together the dry and wet ingredients just until blended. Do not overmix. Divide the batter evenly among the prepared muffin cups, filling them as full as possible.

4. Bake until the muffins spring back when pressed lightly in the center with a fingertip, about 18 minutes. Remove from the oven and immediately turn the muffins out onto a wire rack. Let cool on the rack for a few minutes, then serve warm. The muffins are best when eaten the day they are made.

Pineapple Upside-Down Bran Muffins

These delicious, healthful, almost dessertlike bran muffins were a staple at cafés in Hollywood when I first moved there in the 1980s. They often accompanied large salads like a Cobb or chef's. It turns out that they were a holdover from an earlier era of health-consciousness. According to health food historian, author, and chef Akasha Richmond, bran muffins were promoted by celebrity chef Arthur Wyman as far back as 1927 as a tasty way to get more fiber and whole-grain goodness in diets. **MAKES 12 LARGE OR 18 MEDIUM-SIZED MUFFINS**

TOPPING

⅔ cup firmly packed brown sugar

2 tablespoons unsalted butter, melted

1½ cups pineapple chunks, preferably fresh

MUFFINS

1¾ cups wheat bran

1½ cups unbleached all-purpose flour

½ cup firmly packed brown sugar

1 teaspoon baking powder

1 teaspoon baking soda

½ teaspoon salt

1. Position a rack in the center of the oven and preheat to 375°F. Spray 12 or 18 standard muffin cups generously with nonstick cooking spray.

2. To make the topping, whisk together the brown sugar, butter, and 1 tablespoon water until blended. Divide the mixture evenly among the prepared muffin cups. Spoon an equal amount of the pineapple chunks into each cup.

3. To make the muffins, in a large bowl, whisk together the bran, flour, brown sugar, baking powder, baking soda, and salt. Make a well in the bran mixture and pour in the buttermilk, oil, eggs, molasses, and vanilla. Whisk together the dry and wet ingredients thoroughly yet briefly or the muffins will be tough. Spoon the batter over the pineapple in the muffin cups, dividing it evenly.

4. Bake until the muffins are a deep, rich brown and spring back when pressed lightly in the center with a fingertip, about 25 minutes for 12 muffins or 20 minutes for 18 muffins. The fruit on the bottom makes the muffins feel a bit squishy to the touch, so use your best judgment when testing for doneness. Let cool in the pan on a wire rack for about 5 minutes, then run small offset spatula or a knife around the inside edge of each muffin cup and invert the muffins onto the rack.

1¼ cups buttermilk

⅓ cup canola or other neutral-flavored vegetable oil

2 eggs, lightly beaten

2 tablespoons unsulfured molasses

1 teaspoon vanilla extract

If any of the pineapple chunks slip off, nab them with a fork and return them to the muffins. The chunks will adhere as the muffins cool. Let cool completely before serving. (The muffins can be stored in an airtight container at room temperature for up to 2 days. To keep them longer, wrap tightly and freeze for up to 2 weeks, then thaw for a few hours and reheat in a toaster oven.)

Lemon-Ricotta Muffins

The combination of lemon and ricotta has been a favorite of mine since I first tasted it in a pancake recipe made by my dear friend Nancy Quatrochi. I'll never forget the day I pulled up alongside her on my way to another ten- to twelve-hour bakery workday—on a Sunday no less! She convinced me to make a detour to her place for these pancakes, and they were divine. On the eve of opening my first bakery, she not only painted the walls but also made little fruit paintings to adorn them, and I will be forever grateful. We had no money, and she imbued Mani's Bakery with great charm and character. This recipe is my attempt to capture the experience of her pancakes in a muffin format, right down to the jam served with them in place of syrup.

MAKES 12 MUFFINS

2 cups unbleached all-purpose flour

⅔ cup sugar

2 teaspoons baking powder

½ teaspoon baking soda

¼ teaspoon ground allspice

½ teaspoon salt

½ cup whole-milk or part-skim ricotta cheese

2 eggs

⅔ cup whole milk

½ cup (1 stick) unsalted butter, melted

Grated zest and juice of 1 lemon

⅓ cup preserves such as raspberry, blueberry, or sour cherry

1. Position a rack in the center of the oven and preheat to 375°F. Line a 12-cup standard muffin tin with paper liners.

2. In a medium bowl, whisk together the flour, sugar, baking powder, baking soda, allspice, and salt. In a second medium bowl, whisk together the ricotta, eggs, and milk. Make a well in the flour mixture and pour in the ricotta mixture, butter, and lemon zest and juice. Stir together the dry and wet ingredients with a wooden spoon just until blended. Divide the batter evenly among the prepared muffin cups. Put a heaping teaspoon of preserves in the center of the batter in each cup.

3. Bake until the muffins spring back when pressed lightly near the center with a fingertip, about 18 minutes. Let cool in the pan on a wire rack for 10 to 15 minutes, then lift the muffins out of the pan (using a knife if needed to free them from the cups) and let cool completely on the rack before serving. (The muffins can be stored in an airtight container at room temperature for up to 3 days.)

Morning Glory Muffins

A morning glory muffin is essentially a pared-down carrot cake, loaded with carrots, whole-wheat flour, warm spices, and all sorts of extras like coconut, raisins, and citrus. My first taste of this now-classic muffin came from the pages of The Tassajara Bread Book, *published in 1970. I have reduced the amount of fat and sugar used in the original to satisfy today's higher standards for healthful foods. Freshly grated carrots work best; commercially packaged grated carrots are generally too thick to bake properly.* **MAKES 12 MUFFINS**

1¼ cups whole-wheat pastry flour

1 cup unbleached all-purpose flour

½ teaspoon baking powder

½ teaspoon baking soda

½ teaspoon ground cinnamon

¼ teaspoon ground ginger

½ teaspoon salt

2 eggs, at room temperature

¾ cup firmly packed brown sugar

½ cup whole milk (see note)

½ cup canola or other neutral-flavored vegetable oil

2 cups grated carrots

⅓ cup raisins

½ cup unsweetened shredded or flaked dried coconut, toasted

1 tablespoon freshly squeezed lemon juice

1½ tablespoons grated orange zest

1. Position a rack in the center of the oven and preheat to 350°F. Line a 12-cup standard muffin tin with paper liners or spray with nonstick cooking spray.

2. In a medium bowl, sift together the flours, baking powder, baking soda, cinnamon, ginger, and salt. In a second medium bowl, whisk the eggs for a few minutes until thickened and the color lightens. Add the brown sugar, milk, and oil and whisk until combined. Make a well in the flour mixture and pour in the egg mixture. Stir together with a wooden spoon just until blended. Stir in the carrots, raisins, coconut, lemon juice, and orange zest just until evenly distributed. Divide the batter evenly among the prepared muffin cups.

3. Bake until a toothpick inserted into the center of a muffin comes out clean and the top springs back when pressed lightly in the center with a fingertip, 20 to 25 minutes. Let cool in the pan on a wire rack for 12 to 15 minutes, then turn the muffins out onto the rack. Serve warm or at room temperature. (The muffins can be stored in an air-tight container at room temperature for up to 2 days. To keep them longer, wrap tightly and freeze for up to 2 weeks, then thaw for a few hours at room temperature, split in half, and toast like an English muffin.)

NOTE: Feel free to substitute soy, almond, or coconut milk in place of the cow's milk.

Blueberry Corn Muffins

If you have been seeking a gluten-free recipe that everyone will like—and if you love corn bread—this is the recipe for you. Cornmeal and rice flour tend to be a little on the gritty side, but cornstarch and sour cream help to minimize the grittiness. This recipe yields a dozen large muffins, so be sure to coat both the muffin cups and the top edges of the tin between the cups with butter or cooking spray to ensure successful unmolding. **MAKES 12 LARGE MUFFINS**

1½ cups stone-ground yellow cornmeal

¾ cup rice flour

¾ cup cornstarch

¾ cup sugar

2 teaspoons baking powder

½ teaspoon baking soda

½ teaspoon salt

1 cup whole milk

½ cup sour cream

2 eggs

½ cup (1 stick) unsalted butter, melted

1½ cups fresh or frozen blueberries

1. Position a rack in the center of the oven and preheat to 375°F. Generously butter a 12-cup standard muffin tin or spray with nonstick cooking spray, coating both the muffin cups and the top of the tin.

2. In a large bowl, whisk together the cornmeal, rice flour, cornstarch, sugar, baking powder, baking soda, and salt. In a medium bowl, whisk together the milk, sour cream, and eggs until blended. Make a well in the cornmeal mixture and pour in the egg mixture and the butter. Whisk just until blended. Let the batter sit for about 10 minutes for the cornmeal, flour, and cornstarch to absorb the moisture. Stir in the blueberries. Divide the batter evenly among the prepared muffin cups.

3. Bake until the muffins spring back when pressed lightly in the center with a fingertip, about 24 minutes. Let cool in the pan on a wire rack for about 15 minutes, then turn the muffins out onto the rack. If the muffins will not release from the tin, run a small offset spatula along the inside edge of each cup to loosen the muffin sides, then invert the pan again. Serve warm. These muffins are best when eaten the day they are baked.

Orange & Fig Spelt Muffins

With its healthful content and hearty flavor, spelt flour is one of my favorite baking ingredients. In Italy, cooks have used farro, a close cousin of spelt, for thousands of years, usually milled into flour or simmered as a whole grain in soups, in the same way that Americans cook with wheat berries or barley. On my last trip to Italy, I tasted farro in everything from pasta to focaccia to biscotti, and in each case it was exceptional. Spelt is the closest thing to farro grown here in the United States. It is higher in protein and B vitamins than wheat flour and may be acceptable for people on a low-gluten diet. But it deserves to be appreciated as more than a wheat substitute. These muffins, which include olive oil, figs, and orange zest, have a Mediterranean sensibility. **MAKES 12 MUFFINS**

2¼ cups whole-spelt flour (see note)

⅔ cup sugar

1 teaspoon baking powder

½ teaspoon baking soda

½ teaspoon salt

1 cup buttermilk

⅓ cup plus 1 tablespoon extra-virgin olive oil

2 eggs

¾ cup ¼-inch-diced dried figs

Grated zest of 1 orange

1. Position a rack in the upper third of the oven and preheat to 350°F. Brush a 12-cup standard muffin tin with olive oil or melted butter.

2. In a large bowl, whisk together the flour, sugar, baking powder, baking soda, and salt. In a medium bowl, whisk together the buttermilk, oil, and eggs until well blended. Make a well in the flour mixture and pour in the buttermilk mixture. Using a wooden spoon, stir together the dry and wet ingredients just until blended. Fold in the figs and orange zest, being careful not to overmix. Divide the batter evenly among the prepared muffin cups; the batter should fill the cups.

3. Bake until the muffins spring back when pressed lightly in the center with a fingertip, about 20 minutes. Let cool in the pan on a wire rack for 5 minutes, then turn the muffins out onto the rack. Serve hot or warm. (The muffins can be stored in an airtight container at room temperature for up to 3 days. Reheat in a toaster oven before serving.)

NOTE: Spelt flour is available in natural foods stores and some supermarkets. This recipe was tested with organic whole-grain spelt flour. White or light spelt flour has had much of the bran and germ removed and is similar to unbleached all-purpose flour.

Sunflower Berry Muffins

Sunflower seeds, fresh berries, whole-grain flour, and fruit juice make this muffin as tasty as granola and a lot more fun. Like the spelt flour in the muffins on page 100, flaxseed meal is a powerhouse ingredient that you can easily add to your baking to give it a more healthful profile. It is high in omega-3 fatty acids and fiber, plus it gives baked goods a wonderful texture. These muffins get an extra dividend of vitamins from the apple juice and berries. **MAKES 12 LARGE MUFFINS**

2½ cups whole-wheat pastry flour

1 cup old-fashioned rolled oats

⅔ cup firmly packed brown sugar

¼ cup flaxseed meal (optional)

1½ teaspoons baking soda

1 teaspoon baking powder

½ teaspoon salt

2 eggs

1 cup natural apple, freshly squeezed orange, or white grape juice

½ cup canola or other neutral-flavored vegetable oil

1½ cups fresh or frozen berries such as blueberries, cranberries, raspberries, or blackberries, or a combination

½ cup sunflower seeds

1. Position a rack in the center of the oven and preheat to 375°F. Butter and flour a 12-cup standard muffin tin or spray with nonstick cooking spray.

2. In a large bowl, whisk together the flour, oats, brown sugar, flaxseed meal, baking soda, baking powder, and salt. In a medium bowl, lightly whisk the eggs until blended, then whisk in the fruit juice and oil. Make a well in the flour mixture and pour in the egg mixture. Using a wooden spoon, stir together the dry and wet ingredient just until blended. Fold in the berries and sunflower seeds just until evenly distributed. Divide the batter evenly among the prepared muffin cups.

3. Bake until the muffins spring back when pressed lightly in the center with a fingertip, 22 to 25 minutes. Let cool in the pan on a wire rack for 15 to 20 minutes. Run a small offset spatula along the inside edge of each cup to loosen the muffin sides, then turn the muffins out onto the rack. Serve warm. (The muffins can be stored in an airtight container at room temperature for up to 3 days. Reheat in a toaster oven before serving.)

Honey-Oatmeal Streusel Muffins

If you like oatmeal for breakfast, you'll like these muffins. If you never eat oatmeal for breakfast, these muffins might change your mind. The yogurt and honey help tenderize the whole grains, making this coffee cake-style muffin the perfect addition to nearly any brunch menu. **MAKES 12 MUFFINS**

2 cups whole-wheat pastry flour

1½ cups old-fashioned rolled oats

½ to 1 teaspoon ground cinnamon

½ teaspoon ground nutmeg

1 teaspoon salt

1 teaspoon baking powder

1 teaspoon baking soda

⅓ cup canola or other neutral-flavored vegetable oil

½ cup light-colored honey

2 eggs

1 cup whole-milk or low-fat plain yogurt

4 tablespoons cold unsalted butter, cut into small pieces

3 tablespoons sugar

1. Position a rack in the center of the oven and preheat to 350°F. Line a 12-cup standard muffin tin with paper liners.

2. In a large bowl, whisk together the flour, oats, cinnamon (use the larger amount if you particularly like cinnamon), nutmeg, and salt. Remove ½ cup of this mixture, place it in a small bowl, and reserve for the streusel. Add the baking powder and baking soda to the large bowl and whisk until blended. In a medium bowl, whisk together the oil, honey, eggs, and yogurt until blended. Make a well in the flour mixture in the large bowl and pour in the egg mixture. Whisk together the dry and wet ingredients just until blended. Divide the batter evenly among the prepared muffin cups.

3. To make the streusel, add the butter and sugar to the reserved flour mixture and work them in with your fingers until the mixture forms large, coarse crumbs. Sprinkle the streusel evenly over the filled muffin cups and then press it gently into the batter so that it adheres well during baking.

4. Bake until the muffins spring back when pressed lightly in the center with a fingertip, about 22 minutes. Let cool in the pan on a wire rack for about 20 minutes. Run a small offset spatula or knife along the inside edge of each cup to loosen the muffin sides, then lift the muffins out of the cups onto a serving platter, working carefully so that the streusel does not fall off. Serve warm. (The muffins can be stored in an airtight container at room temperature for up to 3 days. Reheat in a toaster oven before serving.)

Double-Chocolate Raspberry Muffins

These are so cute that my guests called them cupcakes! I adapted an old World War II recipe that called for neither eggs nor butter, because both were in short supply at that time. My vegan friends were thrilled, and no one else suspected that this rich, delectable combination of chocolate and tart raspberries contained no dairy or eggs. Feel free to use frozen raspberries if fresh are unavailable, adding them to the batter frozen. **MAKES 12 MUFFINS**

2⅓ cups unbleached all-purpose flour

1½ cups sugar

½ cup unsweetened cocoa powder

1½ teaspoons baking soda

1 teaspoon salt

¾ cup canola or other neutral-flavored vegetable oil

½ teaspoon distilled white vinegar

2 teaspoons vanilla extract

¾ cup semisweet or milk chocolate chips

1½ cups fresh or frozen raspberries

1. Position a rack in the center of the oven and preheat to 350°F. Line a 12-cup standard muffin tin with paper liners.

2. In a large bowl, whisk together the flour, sugar, cocoa powder, baking soda, and salt. If the mixture is at all lumpy, pass it through a sieve or sifter. In a medium bowl, whisk together the oil, vinegar, vanilla, and 1¼ cups water. Make a well in the flour mixture and gradually pour in the oil mixture, whisking as you go. The mixture will become quite thick and pasty, but you need to whisk firmly so that the dry ingredients absorb all the wet ingredients. Stir in the chocolate chips and about two-thirds of the raspberries. Divide the batter evenly among the prepared muffin cups (see note). Garnish with the remaining raspberries.

3. Bake until the muffins spring back when pressed lightly in the center with a fingertip, 20 to 22 minutes. Let cool in the pan on a wire rack for a few minutes, then turn the muffins out onto the rack and serve warm. These muffins are best when eaten the day they are baked.

NOTE: Sorry, but this recipe makes just a little too much batter for a standard muffin tin! I bake the extra batter in an ovenproof ramekin and enjoy it as a special treat for the baker.

I have memories from every period of my life and a corresponding doughnut, which is funny because I don't eat them all that often. It must be that a good doughnut is quite memorable! Apple fritters (yes, I know, they are not really doughnuts) from the coffee hour after church during my childhood, the honey wheat doughnuts from a dive on Robertson Boulevard in Los Angeles in my twenties, and the late-night excursions to Bob's on Polk Street after moving to San Francisco.

I also owe the humble doughnut a deep debt of gratitude. During the low-fat 1990s, I made a reduced-fat, whole-grain baked doughnut sweetened without sugar, which sounds like it should be awful but somehow wasn't. The prop master of a major movie requested it, I sent a few samples, and I received orders for about twenty dozen over the course of the shoot! The resulting story was picked up by a local weekly and made it all the way to national magazines, which put my new little bakery on the map.

With this chapter, I've updated the old choice between yeast versus cake doughnuts. Now I ask: what's your favorite doughnut, yeast, cake, or baked?

Doughnuts

Brown Sugar–Sour Cherry Doughnuts

I first tasted a cake doughnut with sour cherries at Café Nola on Bainbridge Island, a ferry ride from downtown Seattle. Founder and then-owner Melinda Bulgarin Lucas came up with the brilliant idea of using sour cherries to cut the richness of the doughnuts. I tried to get her recipe but failed, so I have re-created it as closely as possible. It's now an occasional doughnut Sunday special at Sweet Bar Bakery. **MAKES 24 DOUGHNUTS**

4¾ cups unbleached all-purpose flour

1½ teaspoons baking powder

1 teaspoon baking soda

¼ teaspoon salt

¼ teaspoon ground nutmeg

4 tablespoons unsalted butter, at room temperature

¾ cup granulated sugar

½ cup firmly packed brown sugar

2 eggs

1 teaspoon vanilla extract

1 cup buttermilk

1½ cups dried sour (tart) cherries

Canola or other neutral-flavored vegetable oil for deep-frying (about 8 cups)

CINNAMON SUGAR

½ cup granulated sugar

2 teaspoons ground cinnamon

1. In a medium bowl, sift together the flour, baking powder, baking soda, salt, and nutmeg. In a large bowl, using a stand mixer fitted with the paddle attachment or a handheld mixer, cream together the butter and sugars on medium speed until creamy and smooth, about 3 minutes. Add the eggs, one at a time, and beat well after each addition. Add the vanilla and buttermilk and beat until well mixed. Stop the mixer and scrape down the sides of the bowl.

2. On low speed, add the flour mixture and beat just until incorporated. With a wooden spoon, stir in the cherries. Cover the bowl and refrigerate for 30 minutes.

3. Lightly flour a baking sheet. Lightly flour a work surface and turn out the dough onto it. Roll out the dough into a rough disk ½ to ¾ inch thick. Using a 2½-inch round doughnut cutter, cut out as many doughnuts as possible. Transfer the doughnuts and the doughnut holes to the prepared baking sheet. Gather up the dough scraps, gently press them together, pat out the dough ½ to ¾ inch thick, and cut out more doughnuts and holes.

4. Pour the oil to a depth of at least 2½ inches into a wok resting in a secure wok stand or into a heavy-gauge stockpot and heat to 365°F on a deep-frying thermometer. Line a large platter with paper towels.

continued >

5. When the oil is ready, carefully slip 3 or 4 doughnuts into the hot oil and fry, turning them once, until deep golden brown on both sides, about 5 minutes total. Using a slotted spoon or a wire skimmer, transfer the doughnuts to the towel-lined platter to drain and cool for about 4 minutes. Repeat with the remaining doughnuts, always bringing the oil up to temperature before adding the next batch. Fry the doughnut holes separately in two batches; they will be ready in about 2½ minutes.

6. To make the cinnamon sugar, in a small bowl, whisk together the sugar and cinnamon. Using a fine-mesh sieve, dust the warm doughnuts with the cinnamon sugar. Serve the doughnuts warm.

Panfried Apple Fritters with Apple-Honey Dipping Sauce

These fritters lie somewhere between a doughnut and a pancake: less decadent than the former but more decadent than the latter. I consider them cousins to the doughnut and so delicious that you'll probably want to make a double batch. They are especially good with bacon and eggs for breakfast, and because they are panfried, they can be cooked on the spur of the moment. **MAKES ABOUT 15 FRITTERS**

⅔ cup unbleached all-purpose flour

2 teaspoons baking powder

½ teaspoon ground cinnamon

½ teaspoon ground ginger

¼ teaspoon salt

½ cup whole-milk or low-fat plain yogurt

2 eggs, separated

1 tablespoon unsalted butter, melted

2 tablespoons sugar

2 cups peeled, cored, and grated apples such as Granny Smith or Gala

Canola or other neutral-flavored vegetable oil for panfrying

½ cup honey, any kind

1. In a small bowl, whisk together the flour, baking powder, cinnamon, ginger, and salt. In a medium bowl, whisk together the yogurt, egg yolks, butter, and sugar. Add the flour mixture to the yogurt mixture and stir well. Let sit for at least 30 minutes or up to 1 hour.

2. Position a rack in the center of the oven and preheat to 250°F. Line a baking sheet with paper towels.

3. Using your hands, squeeze the grated apples as dry as possible, reserving the juice in a small, heavy saucepan. In a small bowl using a handheld mixer or a hand whisk, whip the egg whites until they form soft, moist peaks. Fold the apples into the yogurt-flour mixture. Add the egg whites and fold in very slowly and gently.

4. Pour the oil to a depth of ¼ inch into a heavy skillet and heat over medium heat. When the oil is hot, drop the batter by the heaping tablespoon into the oil, spreading it gently to a roughly oval shape 2½ to 3 inches long. Avoid pressing or flattening the fritters with a fork and do not crowd the pan. Cook for 2½ to 3 minutes on the first side. Turn the fritters and cook for about 2 minutes on the second side. The fritters should be quite dark. Using tongs or a slotted spatula, transfer them to the towel-lined baking sheet and keep warm in the oven. Repeat with the remaining batter, adding more oil to the pan as needed and always bringing the oil up to temperature before adding the next batch.

5. While the fritters are frying, cook the reserved apple juice over medium-low heat to reduce by three-fourths. Skim off any foam, then add the honey, bring to a boil, and boil for 3 minutes. Pour into a small heatproof serving dish.

6. Serve the fritters hot, with the apple-honey dipping sauce on the side.

Malasadas (Portuguese-Hawaiian Doughnuts)

Malasadas, *which are pillowy on the inside and deliciously craggy and crisp on the outside, should always be eaten just minutes after they emerge from the oil. A specialty of Portuguese Hawaiians, these deep-fried confections were introduced to Hawaii by Portuguese laborers from the Azores and Madeira who came to work in the fields in the late-nineteenth century. In Hawaii, these sweets are traditionally fried to order: you call in your request (at least a dozen—trust me on that!), pick them up when they are fresh and hot, and eat them immediately. The dough is quite sticky, and getting it into the hot oil is a challenge. I recommend that you use a very lightly oiled spoon to slide in about ¼ cup (a roughly 1-inch chunk) of the dough at a time. Hawaiians toss* malasadas *in sugar alone, but if you prefer them mainland style, add a few pinches of ground cinnamon to the sugar.* **MAKES ABOUT 24 DOUGHNUTS**

1 envelope active dry yeast (2¼ teaspoons)

½ cup plus 1 teaspoon sugar, plus 2 cups for coating the doughnuts

6 eggs, at room temperature

4 tablespoons unsalted butter, melted

1 cup evaporated milk

1 teaspoon salt

6 cups unbleached all-purpose flour

Canola or other neutral-flavored vegetable oil for deep-frying (about 8 cups)

1. In a small bowl, sprinkle the yeast and the 1 teaspoon sugar over ¼ cup lukewarm water (100° to 110°F), stir to dissolve, and let stand until foamy, about 5 minutes.

2. In the large bowl of a stand mixer fitted with the whip attachment, beat the eggs until they are pale and have increased in volume, at least 3 minutes. Switch to the dough hook attachment and add the yeast mixture, the ½ cup sugar, the butter, the evaporated milk, 1 cup water, and the salt. Beat on low speed until combined, then begin adding the flour, 1 cup at a time, and beat until the dough begins to come together into a ball. After all the flour is added, continue to knead just until the dough is soft and smooth, about 3 minutes. Form the dough into a ball.

3. Oil a large bowl. Transfer the dough to the bowl, turn the dough to coat on all sides with the oil, and cover the bowl with plastic wrap and a kitchen towel. Let the dough rise in a warm, draft-free spot until doubled in volume, about 1 hour.

continued >

4. When the dough has almost finished rising, pour the oil to a depth of at least 2½ inches into a wok resting in a secure wok stand or into a heavy-gauge stockpot and heat to 365° to 375°F on a deep-frying thermometer. Line a large platter or baking sheet with paper towels and place a large wire rack on the platter or baking sheet.

5. When the oil is ready, using an oiled spoon, scoop up 1-inch pieces of the dough and drop them into the hot oil, frying about 6 doughnuts at a time. Fry, turning them once, until deep golden brown on both sides, 2 to 3 minutes total. Using a slotted spoon or wire skimmer, transfer the doughnuts to the wire rack to drain and cool for about 4 minutes. Repeat with the remaining dough, always bringing the oil up to temperature before adding the next batch of doughnuts.

6. Toss the warm doughnuts in the 2 cups sugar, coating them evenly, and serve warm.

Baked Doughnuts

Commonly known as doughnut muffins, baked doughnuts are very popular in the San Francisco Bay Area. They differ from my fauxnuts (page 119) because they are made from unbleached flour and sugar, just like traditional fried doughnuts, but then they are baked, brushed with melted butter, and tossed in cinnamon sugar. I thought to myself, if you are going to all that trouble, why not just bake them in a mini Bundt molds so they will look like real doughnuts? Feel free to bake them in a muffin tin, if you prefer; you'll need to increase the baking time. Make sure you coat the muffins cups well with cooking spray to ensure the dough-nuts will unmold easily. **MAKES 12 DOUGHNUTS**

4 cups unbleached all-purpose
   flour

1 tablespoon plus ½ teaspoon
   baking powder

1¼ teaspoons salt

1 teaspoon ground nutmeg

½ teaspoon baking soda

1 cup (2 sticks) unsalted butter,
   at room temperature

1 cup plus 2 tablespoons sugar

3 eggs, at room temperature

1¼ cups whole milk

COATING

½ cup (1 stick) unsalted butter

1½ cups sugar

1½ tablespoons ground
   cinnamon

1. Position a rack in the center of the oven and preheat to 350°F. Spray a 6-cup mini Bundt pan with nonstick cooking spray.

2. To make the doughnuts, in a medium bowl, sift together the flour, baking powder, salt, nutmeg, and baking soda. In a large bowl, using a stand mixer fitted with the paddle attachment or a handheld mixer, cream together the butter and sugar on high speed until the mixture is light in color and texture, about 3 minutes. Add the eggs, one at a time, and beat well after each addition.

3. On low speed, add the flour mixture in four batches alternating with the milk in three batches, beginning and ending with the flour mixture and stopping to scrape down the sides of the bowl as needed. The batter should be smooth. Do not overmix. Using half of the batter, fill the prepared molds one-third to one-half full. Do not fill them fuller or the batter may overflow during baking.

4. Bake until the tops spring back when pressed lightly near the center with a fingertip, about 18 minutes. Let cool in the pan on a wire rack for about 10 minutes. Invert the pan, hold it at an angle, and give it a firm whack on the countertop, then repeat the motion until all the dough-nuts pop out. Repeat with the remaining batter, allowing the pan to cool and spraying it with cooking spray before filling and baking.

continued >

5. While the second batch of doughnuts is baking, make the coating. In a small saucepan, melt the butter over low heat, taking care that it does not brown. Remove from the heat. In a medium bowl, whisk together the sugar and cinnamon.

6. Brush the first batch of warm doughnuts all over with the melted butter and then roll each doughnut in the cinnamon-sugar to coat evenly. Transfer to a wire rack, let cool briefly, and then serve warm. Treat the second batch of doughnuts the same way. (You will have leftover cinnamon-sugar, which can be stored in an airtight container and sprinkled on breakfast cereal, used to make cinnamon toast, or stirred into hot beverages. Do not make less cinnamon-sugar, as you need the full amount to coat the doughnuts completely.)

The Original L.A. Fauxnut

These are the doughnuts that made Mani's Bakery famous. Fauxnuts were the answer to a cry for help when Danny DeVito was filming Other People's Money. *His character was addicted to doughnuts, but in real life, the actor did not eat sugar or fried foods. I whipped up a batch of agave syrup–sweetened banana batter, baked it in mini Bundt molds, and rolled the mini "cakes" in a variety of doughnut-style toppings. Dubbed fauxnuts by my dear friend Mary Coller, these were such a hit with Danny and the crew that we quickly added them to the bakery's daily repertoire. The story went viral, and we watched customers line up for them!* **MAKES 12 FAUXNUTS**

3 cups whole-wheat pastry flour

1½ teaspoons baking soda

1 teaspoon salt

½ teaspoon ground cinnamon

1¾ cups mashed ripe bananas

3 eggs

1¾ cups agave syrup, preferably light

¼ cup canola or other neutral-flavored vegetable oil

¼ cup buttermilk

1 teaspoon vanilla extract

SYRUP AND TOPPINGS

1 cup agave syrup, preferably light

Unsweetened shredded dried coconut, graham cracker crumbs, or toasted diced almonds

1. Position a rack in the center of the oven and preheat to 350°F. Spray a 6-cup mini Bundt pan with cooking spray.

2. To make the fauxnuts, in a large bowl, sift together the flour, baking soda, salt, and cinnamon. In a medium bowl, whisk the banana until smooth and creamy. Add the eggs, agave syrup, oil, buttermilk, and vanilla to the banana and whisk until smooth and creamy, about 2 minutes. Make a well in the flour mixture and pour in the banana mixture. Whisk together the dry and wet ingredients briefly yet thoroughly. Fill each mold no more than three-fourths full with batter. The easiest way to do this is to transfer the batter to a liquid measuring cup.

3. Bake until the tops spring back when pressed lightly near the center with a fingertip, 15 to 18 minutes. Let cool in the pan on a wire rack for about 10 minutes. Invert the pan, hold it at an angle, and give it a firm whack on the countertop, then repeat the motion until all the fauxnuts pop out onto the rack. Let the fauxnuts cool completely. Repeat with the remaining batter, allowing the pan to cool and spraying it with cooking spray before filling and baking.

continued >

4. To top the fauxnuts, bring the agave syrup to a low boil over medium heat. Remove from the heat and pour into a small, deep heatproof bowl. Place each of your chosen toppings in a separate small bowl. Turn a cooled fauxnut upside down, dip the top half into the hot syrup, and then roll it in the desired topping. Transfer to a wire rack and repeat with the remaining fauxnuts, then serve at room temperature. Strain the leftover agave syrup to remove any crumbs and save for another purpose.

CHOCOLATE-DIPPED FAUXNUTS: Put 2 cups (12 ounces) semisweet chocolate chips and 1½ teaspoons canola or other neutral-flavored vegetable oil in a heatproof bowl and set over (not touching) hot (not simmering) water in a saucepan. Heat on low, stirring occasionally, until the chocolate is melted and smooth. Remove the bowl from over the water and let cool slightly. Tilt the bowl so the chocolate collects in a deep pool. Turn a cooled fauxnut upside down, dip the top half into the chocolate, and then shake the fauxnut gently so that the excess chocolate drips back into the bowl. Place on a baking sheet and sprinkle with toasted diced almonds or unsweetened shredded dried coconut, if desired. Repeat with the remaining fauxnuts. Refrigerate briefly to set the chocolate before serving.

Full disclosure: I was born on the tail end of the generation that witnessed the first moon orbits, which means I remember the rise of both Tang and Space Food Sticks. We all know Tang, the instant orange juice powder famously used by the astronauts, because that brand is still on store shelves. But Space Food Sticks were first shortened to Food Sticks and then retired completely in the 1980s. My aunt Janet stocked them in her cupboards. We never had them at home, but I could try them on the rare visit to my cousin! The fact that they tasted bad was beside the point. They were marketed on television and were therefore cool. My parents' unwillingness to buy them only increased their allure.

In the 1980s, the granola bar arrived, which was followed by the ubiquitous energy bar, and they both tasted much better.

So the kitchen tinkerer in me has spent a bit of time re-creating granola and cereal bars at home, ones that won't crumble into bits or are overly sweet. I have also worked on what I think are respectable versions of Anzac biscuits (New Zealand and Australia), flapjacks (England), and Italian biscotti. If only the astronauts could eat so well.

Bars & Cookies

Hi-NRG Peanut Butter Breakfast Cookies

Protein for breakfast is on the rise! If you are somebody who starts your day better with a jolt of protein than with a dose of carbohydrates, this is for you. The peanut butter alone packs in a whopping seventy-two grams of protein, about three grams per serving. Add in whole-grain oats and flour, and you have a great way to begin the day or power up for a workout. Customize with your choice of sweet (chocolate), salty (pretzel bits), or superfood (pomegranate). **MAKES 24 LARGE COOKIES**

1½ cups whole-wheat pastry flour

1½ cups old-fashioned rolled oats

½ teaspoon baking soda

½ teaspoon salt

¾ cup (1½ sticks) unsalted butter, at room temperature, or coconut oil

½ cup granulated sugar

1 cup firmly packed brown sugar

1 cup creamy peanut butter (see note)

2 eggs

1 teaspoon vanilla extract

¾ cup milk chocolate or semi-sweet chocolate chips, smashed pretzel bits, or dried pomegranate seeds

1. Position a rack in the upper third and a second rack in the lower third of the oven and preheat to 350°F. Line 2 baking sheets with parchment paper or nonstick baking mats.

2. In a medium bowl, whisk together the flour, oats, baking soda, and salt. In a large bowl, using a stand mixer fitted with the paddle attachment or a handheld mixer, combine the butter, sugars, peanut butter, eggs, and vanilla and beat on medium speed until creamy, about 2 minutes. On low speed, add the flour mixture, then increase the speed to medium and beat just until well blended. Stir in the chocolate chips.

3. Using an ice cream scoop or a large spoon, scoop up the dough and drop it onto the prepared baking sheets, placing 12 equal-sized mounds on each sheet and spacing them evenly apart. Using the tines of a fork dipped into water, shape and flatten each dough mound into an oval.

4. Bake the cookies, switching the pans between the racks and rotating them back to front about halfway through baking, until they are nicely browned, about 14 minutes. Transfer the cookies to a wire rack and let cool completely. (The cookies can be stored in an airtight container at room temperature for up to 10 days.)

NOTE: I recommend creamy natural peanut butter, with no added oils, sugar, or partially hydrogenated fats. Stir in the naturally separated peanut oil before using.

Apple-Oatmeal Triangles (Flapjacks)

To an American, flapjacks are pancakes, but to the British, a flapjack is a chewy oat bar with toffee notes. In the British Isles, they are often made with treacle or golden syrup. My version combines brown sugar and golden syrup for a more complex flavor and adds an apple layer. Honey is a perfectly acceptable substitute if golden syrup is hard to find, but the cookies will be crumblier. Many people will appreciate the fact that these cookies are gluten-free and whole grain. **MAKES 8 WEDGE-SHAPED COOKIES**

2 large cooking apples such as Fuji, Rome, or Granny Smith, peeled, cored, and diced

2 tablespoons peeled and grated fresh ginger

1 tablespoon freshly squeezed lemon juice

½ cup (1 stick) unsalted butter

½ cup firmly packed light brown sugar

3 tablespoons golden syrup or honey

2½ cups old-fashioned rolled oats

½ cup sliced almonds

½ teaspoon ground cinnamon

¼ teaspoon salt

1. Position a rack in the center of the oven and preheat to 375°F. Butter a 9-inch pie pan.

2. In a small saucepan, combine the apples, ginger, lemon juice, and 3 tablespoons water and bring to a simmer over medium heat. Reduce the heat to low and simmer, stirring occasionally and adding a little more water if the mixture seems dry, until the apples are very tender, about 10 minutes. Set aside to cool.

3. In a medium saucepan, combine the butter, brown sugar, and golden syrup over low heat and heat, stirring a few times, just until the butter is melted. Do not let the mixture come to a boil. Add the oats, almonds, cinnamon, and salt and stir well. Press half the oats mixture in the prepared pan. Spread the apple puree evenly over the top and cover with the remaining oats mixture.

4. Bake until the top is golden brown, 28 to 30 minutes. Remove from the oven and mark into 8 wedges while still warm. (This will make it easier to cut the flapjacks once they have cooled.) Set the pan on a wire rack and let cool completely. Slice through the marks to cut into wedges and serve directly from the pan. (The flapjacks can be stored in an airtight container at room temperature for up to 3 days.)

Cranberry-Almond Breakfast Bars

Most people automatically buy packaged mass-produced breakfast bars, but these handy treats are surprisingly easy to make, and homemade bars taste much better than store-bought. With this recipe, you'll get a dozen bars that are ideal for breakfast on the run. Each one is packed with fiber from whole-wheat flour, oats, and flaxseeds; protein from almonds; and antioxidant-rich cranberries. **MAKES 12 BARS**

1 cup whole-wheat flour

1 cup old-fashioned rolled oats

¼ cup flaxseeds

½ teaspoon baking powder

½ teaspoon baking soda

¼ teaspoon salt

½ cup orange juice, preferably freshly squeezed

½ cup firmly packed light brown sugar

1 egg, lightly beaten

2 tablespoons canola or other neutral-flavored vegetable oil

1 cup sliced or chopped almonds

½ cup dried cranberries

1. Position a rack in the center of the oven and preheat to 350°F. Brush an 8-inch square baking pan with oil or melted butter.

2. In a large bowl, whisk together the flour, oats, flaxseeds, baking powder, baking soda, and salt. Make a well in the flour mixture and add the orange juice, brown sugar, egg, and oil. Whisk just until combined. Stir in the almonds and cranberries.

3. Spread the batter evenly in the prepared pan. Using a knife, cut the moist dough into thirds. Rotate the pan a quarter turn and cut the dough into fourths to make 12 bars total. (Cutting the bars now will make it easier to cut through and separate the bars after baking.)

4. Bake until the top is lightly browned, 24 to 28 minutes. Let cool completely in the pan on a wire rack. Invert the pan onto a cutting board and lift off the pan, leaving the baked slab on the board. Using the previous cuts as a guide and a large, sharp knife, cut the slab into bars. (The bars can be stored in an airtight container at room temperature for up to 5 days. Or, wrap each bar individually in plastic wrap and then aluminum foil and freeze for up to 3 months. Thaw at room temperature overnight.)

Blueberry Crumble Bars

Here is an ideal recipe for a summer day when blueberries are coming into season. (In winter, you can use frozen berries; add them to the batter frozen.) This recipe uses a standard loaf pan and yields just 6 bars. If you want to make more, you can double the recipe and use a 9-by-13-inch baking pan. The baking time for the bottom crust will remain the same, but you will need to add 10 minutes or so to the second baking time.

MAKES 6 LARGE BARS

FILLING

1½ **cups fresh or frozen blueberries**

⅓ **cup firmly packed brown sugar**

1½ **teaspoons cornstarch**

1 **teaspoon grated lemon zest**

CRUMBLE CRUST

¾ **cup old-fashioned rolled oats**

¾ **cup unbleached all-purpose flour**

½ **cup firmly packed brown sugar**

½ **teaspoon baking powder**

¼ **teaspoon salt**

6 **tablespoons unsalted butter, melted**

1. To make the filling, in a small saucepan, combine the blueberries, brown sugar, and ⅓ cup water and bring to a boil, stirring occasionally to dissolve the sugar. Lower the heat to a simmer and cook for 3 minutes.

2. In a small bowl, whisk together the cornstarch and 2 tablespoons water until the cornstarch has dissolved. Add to the simmering berries and cook, stirring frequently, for 2 to 3 minutes. Remove from the heat, stir in the lemon zest, and let cool.

3. Position a rack in the center of the oven and preheat to 350°F. Have ready a 9-by-5-by-3-inch loaf pan.

4. To make the crust, in a medium bowl, stir together the oats, flour, brown sugar, baking powder, and salt. Using a wooden spoon, stir the butter into the oats mixture. Spread half the mixture evenly in the loaf pan and pack it down firmly with your fingers. Bake for 15 minutes and let cool briefly.

5. Pour the cooled blueberry mixture over the prebaked crust and sprinkle the remaining crust mixture evenly over the top. Bake until the crust is deep brown and the filling has bubbled up through it a bit, 30 to 35 minutes. Transfer to a wire rack to cool. As the layers cool, the fruit filling will thicken. Cut into bars to serve. Served warm, the bars will be runny but tasty. Serve at room temperature; the filling will have set nicely. (The bars can be covered and stored at room temperature for up to 2 days or refrigerated for up to 5 days.)

Big Almond-Cherry Biscotti

Tart cherries, cinnamon, and lime complement the toasty aroma of whole almonds in these crisp, dunkable cookies. If you like, dip the finished biscotti in melted chocolate. You can either coat the flat bottom of each cookie, or you can dip each one halfway into the chocolate. To prepare the chocolate, follow the directions for chocolate-dipped fauxnuts on page 120. **MAKES ABOUT 32 BISCOTTI**

1¾ cups unbleached all-purpose flour

¾ cup sugar

1½ teaspoons baking powder

½ teaspoon ground cinnamon

½ teaspoon salt

4 tablespoons cold unsalted butter, cut into small pieces

3 eggs, lightly beaten

1½ teaspoons vanilla extract

Grated zest and juice of 1 large or 2 small limes

1½ cups whole raw almonds

⅔ cup dried sour (tart) cherries or cranberries

1 egg beaten with 1 tablespoon water for glaze

1. Position one rack in the center and a second rack in the upper third of the oven and preheat to 350°F. Line 2 baking sheets with parchment paper or nonstick baking mats.

2. In a medium bowl, whisk together the flour, sugar, baking powder, cinnamon, and salt. Scatter the butter over the flour mixture. Using your fingers or a pastry cutter, work in the butter until the mixture resembles large coarse crumbs. Add the eggs and the lime zest and juice and, using your hands or a wooden spoon, mix just until the mixture forms a stiff dough. Add the almonds and cherries and work them into the dough until evenly distributed.

3. Lightly flour a work surface and transfer the dough to it. Divide the dough in half. Shape each half into a log about 9 inches long and 2 inches in diameter. Place the logs on a prepared baking sheet, spacing them as far apart as possible. Brush the tops and sides with the glaze.

4. Bake on the center rack of the oven until the logs are golden and set but are still somewhat soft to the touch, 20 to 25 minutes. Remove from the oven and reduce the oven temperature to 300°F. Let the logs cool on the pan on a wire rack for 10 minutes. Set the lined baking sheet aside.

5. Transfer the logs to a cutting board. Using a serrated knife and a light touch, cut the logs on a slight diagonal into ½-inch-thick slices. Arrange the slices, curved sides up and ½ inch apart, on the 2 prepared baking sheets.

6. Bake until the biscotti are golden and crisp, about 30 minutes. Let cool completely on the pans on wire racks. The biscotti will firm up and dry as they cool. (The biscotti can be stored in an airtight container at room temperature for up to 2 weeks.)

Biscotti di Meliga (Cornmeal Biscotti)

I fell in love with the variety of shapes, sizes, tastes, and textures of the little biscotti served in the Piedmont region of northern Italy with cappuccino, even at breakfast! I use a coarse-grind cornmeal here for both flavor and texture, but you can use a finer grind if you like. Some bakers pipe the dough onto the baking sheets, but I roll it by hand into small logs. Marking the logs with the tines of a fork makes them look like cute little ears of corn. Traditionally, lemon zest is added to the dough, but I prefer lime, so you can choose your favorite. This recipe is easily doubled. **MAKES ABOUT 18 BISCOTTI**

¾ cup (1½ sticks) unsalted butter, at room temperature

½ cup sugar

2 egg yolks

1 teaspoon grated lime or lemon zest

1 cup unbleached all-purpose flour

⅔ cup coarse-grind stone-ground yellow cornmeal

1. In a medium bowl, using a stand mixer fitted with the paddle attachment or a handheld mixer, cream together the butter and sugar on medium speed until creamy and smooth, about 3 minutes. Add the egg yolks and beat until fully incorporated. Toss in the lime zest and beat just until combined. Using a wooden spoon, stir the flour and cornmeal into the butter mixture until combined.

2. Knead the mixture a few times in the bowl until it comes together. Cover the bowl with a kitchen towel and let stand for 1 hour. This will help the cornmeal to absorb moisture.

3. Position a rack in the center of the oven and preheat to 325°F. Line 2 baking sheets with parchment paper or nonstick baking mats.

4. To form each cookie, scoop up 1½ tablespoons of the dough and roll between your fingers into a little log. As you form the logs, arrange them on a prepared baking sheet, spacing them evenly apart. When the baking sheet is full, run the tines of a fork firmly but gently over the surface of each log. Patch together any bits of dough that come off each cookie to make additional cookies.

5. When the first baking sheet is full, place it in the oven and bake the biscotti just until they are golden around the edges, 16 to 18 minutes. Transfer the biscotti to a wire rack and let cool completely. Bake and cool the second pan the same way. (The cookies can be stored in an airtight container at room temperature for up to 1 week.)

Wildflower Honey Cereal Bars

The flour, egg, and juice separate this from a heavy, grainy granola bar, and the addition of your favorite cereal makes them light and crispy. Use any cereal that appeals to you. I couldn't decide between Cheerios and Rice Krispies, so I used both! **MAKES 15 BARS**

1 cup whole-wheat flour

1 cup old-fashioned rolled oats

1 cup cereal such as Rice Krispies, Cheerios, or even Lucky Charms

¼ cup flaxseeds

½ teaspoon baking powder

½ teaspoon baking soda

¼ teaspoon ground cinnamon

¼ teaspoon ground nutmeg

¼ teaspoon salt

½ cup wildflower or other honey of choice

1 egg

⅓ cup natural apple juice

4 tablespoons canola or other neutral-flavored vegetable oil or melted unsalted butter

1 teaspoon vanilla extract

1 cup chopped almonds or walnuts or whole sunflower seeds

½ cup chopped dried fruit such as cherries, apricots, or cranberries

1. Position a rack in the center of the oven and preheat to 350°F. Brush an 8-inch square pan with butter or coat with nonstick cooking spray.

2. In a large bowl, whisk together the flour, oats, cereal, flaxseeds, baking powder, baking soda, cinnamon, nutmeg, and salt. In a small bowl, whisk together the honey and egg until blended, then whisk in the apple juice, oil, and vanilla. Make a well in the flour mixture and pour in the honey mixture. Whisk together the dry and wet ingredients just until blended. Stir in the nuts and dried fruit.

3. Spread the batter evenly in the prepared pan. Using a knife, cut the moist dough into thirds. Rotate the pan a quarter turn and cut the dough into fifths to make 15 bars total. (Cutting the bars now will make it easier to cut through and separate the bars after baking.)

4. Bake until the tops of the bars are lightly browned, about 22 minutes. Let cool in the pan on a wire rack for about 15 minutes. Using the previous cuts as a guide and a large, sharp knife, cut into bars, then transfer the bars to the rack and let cool completely. (The bars can be stored in an airtight container at room temperature for up to 5 days. Or, wrap each bar individually in plastic wrap, slip the bars into a zip-top bag, and freeze for up to 3 months. Thaw at room temperature overnight.)

Anzac Biscuits

These wonderful coconut and oat confections manage to be both crisp and chewy, thanks to the golden syrup in the batter. Look for the syrup in the baking section of well-stocked grocery stores. It is well worth seeking out!

Anzac is an acronym for Australia and New Zealand Army Corps. These long-keeping treats date back to World War I, when they were tucked into care packages for soldiers. They are so beloved that the name is protected by the governments of the two countries to keep the recipe from being referred to as anything other than Anzac biscuits. **MAKES ABOUT 24 COOKIES**

1 cup old-fashioned rolled oats

1 cup unbleached all-purpose flour

1 cup unsweetened shredded or flaked dried coconut

⅔ cup sugar

½ cup (1 stick) unsalted butter

2 tablespoons golden syrup

2 tablespoons boiling water

1 teaspoon baking soda

1. Position one rack in the center and a second rack in the upper third of the oven and preheat to 350°F. Line 2 baking sheets with parchment paper or nonstick baking mats.

2. In a large bowl, stir together the oats, flour, coconut, and sugar. In a medium saucepan, melt the butter over medium heat. Add the golden syrup and stir to combine. In a small cup, stir together the boiling water and baking soda, add to the butter mixture, and stir well. Pour the butter mixture into the oats mixture and mix with a wooden spoon or rubber spatula until the dough pulls together.

3. To form each biscuit, scoop up a heaping tablespoon of the dough, shape it into a ball, and then flatten it between your palms into a disk 1½ inches in diameter. As the cookies are formed, place them on the baking sheets, spacing them 1 inch apart.

4. Bake the cookies, switching the pans between the racks and rotating them back to front about halfway through baking, until they turn a deep orange-brown, 12 to 15 minutes. Let cool on the pans on wire racks for a few minutes, then carefully transfer the cookies to the racks and let cool completely. (The cookies can be stored in an airtight container at room temperature for up to 2 weeks.)

Many morning baked goods taste even better when paired with fresh fruit captured in a saucy spread. This little primer includes half a dozen spreads to slather on the recipes in this book, to use as a sauce or plate garnish, or to dress up toast or English muffins. Choose fruits that are at the height of their season for the best results. All the recipes are simple and quick to assemble, and none of them calls for sterilized jars or a hot-water bath. The yield for each recipe is relatively small—just enough to last the better part of a week and to share with weekend guests.

Spreads

Balsamic-Glazed Figs

Choose plump, ripe figs—Black Mission or Brown Turkey is a good choice—for this luxurious spread. **MAKES ABOUT 2 CUPS**

2 tablespoons unsalted butter

¼ cup firmly packed brown sugar

3 tablespoons light-colored honey

2 tablespoons balsamic vinegar

1 pound ripe fresh figs, stemmed and quartered, or diced if large

1. In a heavy skillet, combine the butter, brown sugar, and honey over medium to medium-high heat, bring to a simmer, and cook, stirring constantly, until melted and bubbly, 3 to 4 minutes. Add the vinegar (you may want to turn on the fan; cooking vinegar can release an intense smell) and continue to cook, stirring constantly, until a thickened glaze forms, about 2 minutes longer.

2. Add the figs and toss to coat evenly with the glaze. Continue cooking, stirring often, until the figs soften, 4 to 5 minutes longer. Remove from the heat and serve warm or at room temperature. Or, transfer to an airtight container and refrigerate for up to 5 days.

Ginger-Spiced Applesauce

The combination of ginger and apple makes me think of farm stands and autumn. This applesauce is delicious on its own, or spooned over tea cakes or Mexican Breakfast Bread Pudding. **MAKES ABOUT 1½ CUPS**

2 large cooking apples such as Fuji, Rome, or Granny Smith, peeled, cored, and diced

2 tablespoons peeled and grated fresh ginger

1 tablespoon freshly squeezed lemon juice

1. In a small saucepan, combine the apples, ginger, lemon juice, and 3 tablespoons water and bring to a simmer over medium heat. Reduce the heat to low and simmer, stirring occasionally and adding a little more water if the mixture seems too dry, until the apples are very tender, about 10 minutes.

2. Remove from the heat and mash the apples a little, leaving the mixture slightly chunky. Serve warm or at room temperature. Or, transfer to an airtight container and refrigerate for up to 5 days.

Lemon Mascarpone Cream

This lemony cream is a wonderful alternative to jams or preserves and to more intensely flavored lemon curd. Serve on slices of Lemon–Poppy Seed Bundt Cake. **MAKES 1 GENEROUS CUP**

2 ounces cream cheese, at room temperature

3 tablespoons sugar

8 ounces mascarpone cheese

1 teaspoon vanilla extract

Grated zest and juice of 1 lemon

3 to 4 tablespoons heavy cream (optional)

1. In a medium bowl, using a rubber spatula or wooden spoon, gently mix together the cream cheese and sugar until well blended. Fold in the mascarpone, vanilla, and lemon zest and juice until evenly combined. Cover and refrigerate until serving; it will keep for up to 3 days.

2. For a smoother consistency, fold in the cream just before serving.

Orange Honey Butter

Growing up, I couldn't imagine corn bread or biscuits without honey butter. I still swoon when fancy restaurants serve it, even though it is so easy to make. **MAKES ABOUT 1¼ CUPS**

¾ cup (1½ sticks) cold unsalted butter, cut into tablespoon-sized chunks

½ cup honey, any kind

Grated zest of 1 orange (4 to 5 teaspoons)

1. Leave the butter at room temperature long enough for it to become pliable but not too soft. In a medium bowl, using a stand mixer fitted with the whip attachment or a handheld mixer, whip together the butter and honey on medium speed for 1 to 2 minutes, increasing the speed as they begin to blend together. Alternatively, combine the butter and honey in a medium bowl and fold and mash them together with a wooden spoon. The soft, viscous honey and the cool butter will emulsify to the perfect spreading consistency.

2. Mix in the orange zest to taste, adding 1 to 2 teaspoons at a time and tasting as you go. Spoon the honey butter into a ramekin and serve. Or, cover tightly and store at room temperature for up to 4 days or refrigerate for up to 1 week.

Roasted Plums

This recipe works well with almost any fruit or combination of fruits: apples and blueberries in the fall, pears and cranberries in the winter, just about any stone fruit in the summer. Just remember, the wine will turn everything red, so select your fruits with that in mind. **MAKES ABOUT 1¼ CUPS**

6 to 8 ripe plums, halved, pitted, and sliced (about 3 cups)

½ cup red wine such as Pinot Noir, Merlot, or Zinfandel

⅓ cup firmly packed light brown sugar

1. Position a rack in the center of the oven and preheat to 425°F.

2. Combine the plums, wine, and brown sugar in an earthenware or glass baking dish and stir to mix. Bake for about 30 minutes, or until the plums are tender and the sauce is slightly thickened

3. Transfer to a serving dish and serve warm or at room temperature.

Strawberry-Rhubarb Preserves

These preserves evoke the taste of spring and summer. Spread some on coffee cakes, scones, and muffins to add an extra dimension of flavor. **MAKES ABOUT 1¾ CUPS**

½ cup sugar

1 tablespoon cornstarch or tapioca starch

3 cups sliced rhubarb (¼-inch-wide slices)

1 cup sliced strawberries (⅓-inch-thick slices)

1. In a small bowl, whisk together the sugar and cornstarch. In a small nonreactive saucepan, combine the rhubarb, strawberries, and ½ cup water and bring to a simmer over medium-low heat. Cook for about 3 minutes, stirring occasionally. Add the sugar-cornstarch mixture and continue cooking, stirring constantly, until the cornstarch is no longer cloudy and the fruit looks translucent, about 3 minutes. If the mixture becomes too dry or thick as it cooks, add more water, 1 tablespoon at a time.

2. Transfer to a serving dish and serve warm or at room temperature. Or, transfer to an airtight container and refrigerate for up to 4 days.

Index